THE BOOK OF VINTAGE BOARD GAMES

THE BOOK OF
VINTAGE
BOARD GAMES

HISTORY AND ENTERTAINMENT
FROM THE LATE 18TH TO
THE BEGINNING OF THE 20TH CENTURY

Text and photos by

Adrian Seville

mango
PUBLISHING GROUP

J. VLIEGER - AMSTERDAM.

Contents

Game of Harlequin. Amsterdam: Vlieger, about 1890

Introduction

*B*oard games first appeared in print at the end of the sixteenth century, with games like the Game of the Goose – a simple race game played with dice, as detailed in Chapter 1 of this book – making their way from Italy to other parts of Europe. Initially, these games featured basic designs and were printed on delicate paper. However, the printed board game saw unprecedented levels of creativity and elegance during the nineteenth century. In fact, the century kicked off with a golden era for high-end board games, intricately engraved and frequently adorned with radiant hand-coloring. But these upscale games soon faced stiff competition from the emerging lithography technique, and by the century's close, mass-produced games from steam presses were saturating the pan-European market. Themes of these games spanned a broad spectrum, from serious subjects like geography or history to the latest fads. Gameplay often depended on dice or a small, numbered spinning top known as a totum (or teetotum), offering players no decision in movement. Today, the allure of these games isn't so much in playing them – though many remain entertaining – but in recognizing how they mirror the unique cultures of varying eras and locales. Some games were crafted for gambling, with one victorious player claiming all the stakes. Others, however, were designed as 'mind games,' demanding deep contemplation.

This book showcases examples from all these categories and features games from a diverse array of countries – England, France, Germany, The Netherlands, Belgium, Spain, and the USA. It's intriguing to observe how the emphasis of the games evolved over the century and beyond. For instance, the Game of the Goose, which served as a template for numerous games, was tailored to new markets. What was primarily a gambling game for adults transitioned into a children's game intended for family fun. Also geared for family use were instructional and moral games, crafted to mold the character of the youth. As travel became more accessible and cost-effective throughout the century, games symbolizing journeys underwent transformations. Stagecoaches gave way to trains and steamboats. And as tourism expanded, games that once echoed the aristocrat's Grand Tour transitioned to ones like the Tour of Switzerland, a sought-after destination. Games mirroring recreational activities flourished and diversified greatly. On the other hand, games with a satirical bent or a potent political undertone persisted throughout the century and were certainly not kid-friendly. Such games adeptly employed imagery to relay their message, paralleling the rise of promotional games that emerged late in the century and diversified into the next. Excluded from this book are instances of board games like chess or checkers. By the century's end, it became more economical to print these boards in color instead of crafting them from wood or alternative materials.

While the primary focus of this book zeroes in on the wealth of European games, the concluding chapter delves into how these games whetted the appetite for games in the United States. The games circulating in the U.S. during the early 1800s primarily hailed from London. Advertisements across cities like New York, Boston, or Philadelphia consistently spotlighted the 'latest game' in vogue. Even when homegrown American games began emerging, they typically took cues from well-known European counterparts, although this inspiration wasn't always credited. In fact, one of the most celebrated American games, the Mansion of Happiness, first released by Ives in 1843, discreetly adapts a London game

from the early 19th century. Yet, as the century progressed, American innovation took center stage. This shift was epitomized in 1860 with Milton Bradley's Checkered Game of Life, which pivoted the societal influence of board games.

A notable aspect of the games featured in this book is how vividly they capture the distinct cultures from which they emerged. Nearly every game boasts a plethora of intricate illustrations ripe for examination from various angles. Attire, commonplace items, professions, and recreational activities all present abundant showcases emblematic of their respective nations and epochs. However, delving deeper into these games can unveil intricate and occasionally unsettling socio-cultural sentiments. Readers eager to dive into a detailed exploration of these games are encouraged to visit the Italian website spearheaded by Dr. Luigi Ciompi and the author – www.giochidelloca.it. This site provides high-resolution images of over 2,500 board games, available for free download for personal use. Additionally, an exhaustive bibliography and an ample assortment of articles are accessible for those keen on delving further into the allure of these captivating and aesthetically pleasing games.

The Game of the Goose and Other Animals

The medieval Game of the Goose – a swift and intense race game popular all over Europe – underwent a transformation in the nineteenth century. Often, animals, especially monkeys mocking human behavior, substituted for the geese, adding a unique comedic element to the game.

Perhaps the Game of the Goose is the most seminal of all printed board games. It has given birth to literally thousands of variants throughout the centuries – all straightforward dice games played on a spiraled track with no option of movement, but spanning a vast array of themes. To this day, the game continues to be played, with new variations still emerging, particularly in the Netherlands.

Its earliest mentions trace back to fifteenth-century Italy, mostly as counsel against its play or even as legal bans – a clear indicator of its popularity. The game's association with gambling stirred this disapproval. In fact, when Francesco de' Medici gifted the game to the Court of Philip II of Spain in the late sixteenth century, Philip's jester,

'Gonzalillo,' lamentably wrote to Francesco, 'Cursed be your servant, Luis Dovara, who brought this diabolic game known as Gioco dell'Oca [Game of the Goose], played with two dice... Played in Tuscany, may the creator be damned for the Prince, the Infanta, and Luis Tristan have lost 40 scudi due to it.' *The game's popularity radiated across Europe during this period, primarily through print, and it remained a beloved pastime for two centuries. To grasp its enduring appeal, consider the New and Entertaining Children's Game of the Goose, tailored for the young ones in the Netherlands. While branded as 'new,' this version and its regulations would resonate deeply with Gonzalillo and the Spanish Court. This 'classic' rendition, barring minor rule tweaks, would have been universally recognized throughout Western Europe.*

Upon inspecting the game, its namesake becomes clear: geese are prominently featured across the game's track. Why geese? They're likely symbols of luck in Italy, and in the game, geese typically herald good fortune. Landing on a goose space allows the player to roll again, doubling their move. Players utilize two dice, and with a track spanning just 63 spaces, it makes for a dynamic game. However, there's an intriguing nuance: rolling a nine initially could, in theory, let a player jump from goose to goose and win instantly. To counter this, a unique rule is applied to an initial roll of nine, sending the player either to space 26 or 53, depending on the specific dice combination. This doesn't guarantee victory, but it's indeed an auspicious roll, especially landing on space 53 where the next roll could be a winning one.

Yet, clinching the final space isn't typically straightforward. Numerous pitfalls exist, where the unlucky player must forfeit a stake to the winner's pool. While stakes can range in value, children often wager with candies, nuts, or tiny cookies. Among the hazards, death (space 58) is the most dreaded as players must start over. But spaces like the well and the prison also spell trouble: there, a player remains stuck until another player arrives to take their place. An appealing aspect of the game is that overshooting the last space results In moving backward by the extra points, adding an element of suspense.

From a broader perspective, the game can be perceived as an allegory for human life. The geese might signify fortuitous events or possibly divine interventions on a spiritual journey, whereas the obstacles symbolize life's challenges. Delving deeper into symbolism, for instance, the bridge at space 6 might signify the transition into adulthood, while other spaces carry specific interpretations. This kind of interpretation, especially considering the game's medieval origins in a time when symbolism was prevalent, isn't far-fetched. Even the game's numerology, like the victory number 63 associated with a significant life crisis, supports this allegorical view. By the nineteenth century, however, these philosophical interpretations had faded into obscurity, and the Game of the Goose was enjoyed simply as a game.

REGLEMENT OP HET VERNIEUWD VERMAKELIJK KINDER GANZE

I. Men neemt twee dobbelsteenen, welke aan alle zijde met oogen geteekend zijn.

II. Men werpt met de steenen, wie eerst fpeelt.

III. Die in het begin, of de eerfte reis, 6 en 3 oogen werpt gaat tot No. 26, en die 5 en 4 oogen werpt, zet zich op No. 53.

IV. Die werpt, dat hij op een GANS komt, mag nog weder voortellen, zoo veel oogen als hij heeft geworpen, tot dat hij komt, daar waar geen GANS ftaat.

V. Die werpt dat hij op de BRUG komt, betaald, doch die dubbeld betalen wil, gaat tot No. 12.

VI. Die werpt, dat hij in de HERBERG komt, moet zijn gelag betalen, en zijn beurt ééns laten voorbij gaan.

VII. Die werpt, dat hij in de PUT komt, moet betalen, en zoo lang blijven ftaan, tot dat hij van een ander verlost word.

VIII. Die werpt dat hij in den DOOLHO komt, moet betalen en drie oogen weder ter tellen.

IX. Die werpt, dat hij in de GEVANGEN komt, moet fluitgeld betalen, en zoo lang blij ven, tot dat hij weder van een ander verlo word.

X. Die werpt dat hij op de DOOD kom moet betalen en weder op nieuw, van vor af beginnen te fpelen.

Te Zalt-Bommel, bij JOHANNES NOMAN, Boekdrukker.

che Jeugd.

an een ander achterhaald, en op
mer komt, betaald en gaat op
mmer terug.
erpt, dat hij op over 63 komt,
overig getal zoo veel terug, en
en GANS valt, moet hij nog zoo
en.
n 63 werpt, wint de geheele pot,
er eerst.

*New and entertaining Children's
Game of the Goose, for the
Youth of the Netherlands.
Zalt-Bommel: Noman
about 1825*

Despite its allure, by the start of the nineteenth century, the Game of the Goose was seen as outdated, at least by adults. This perception marked the beginning of its evolution into a game predominantly for children. A notable indication of this transition is a version from the Netherlands, characterized by a central illustration that depicts young individuals engrossed in the game. The sheer intensity is palpable - the boy on the left appears almost too anxious to watch. This iteration of the game is beautifully engraved, most notably showcasing a striking image of Death on space 58, confidently marching with his scythe slung over his shoulder. Subsequent children's editions of the game often opted for a milder representation in the death space. Instead of the traditional garden of paradise, the winning space in this version prominently displays a 'horn of plenty.'

Game of the Goose.
Épinal: Pinot & Sagaire
about 1860

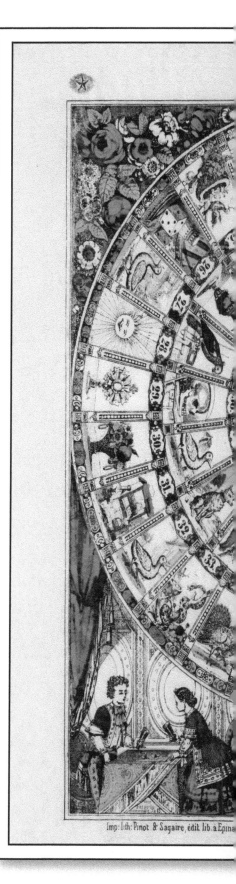

Although the subsequent game, a French version from around 1860, appears markedly different from the Dutch game, it remains a rendition of the classic Game of the Goose, or 'Jeu de l'oie' in French. The primary distinction lies in the non-active spaces; previously empty, they now boast vibrant illustrations. These enhancements aim to elevate the game's appeal. However, they inadvertently create visual competition with the active spaces, such as the geese and hazards, which can make gameplay somewhat challenging. In this version, the depicted scenes on the track lack a cohesive theme and are merely for children's amusement. In the bottom left corner, an illustration portrays a young man challenging a girl: 'You lose, mademoiselle – I have 63!' This game originated from Épinal, a provincial region in northeastern France, which became renowned for its mass production of printed visuals. This encompassed not only games but also a myriad of popular prints, elevating it to a significant global industry. The production value of the game is modest, utilizing affordable, machine-made paper. The color application appears rudimentary, with individual stencils for each hue dabbed on using a *pochoir*, a small cloth pad. Playing tokens are printed on the side, designed to be snipped out and assembled.

Imp: lith: Pinot & Sagaire, édit. lib. à Epinal

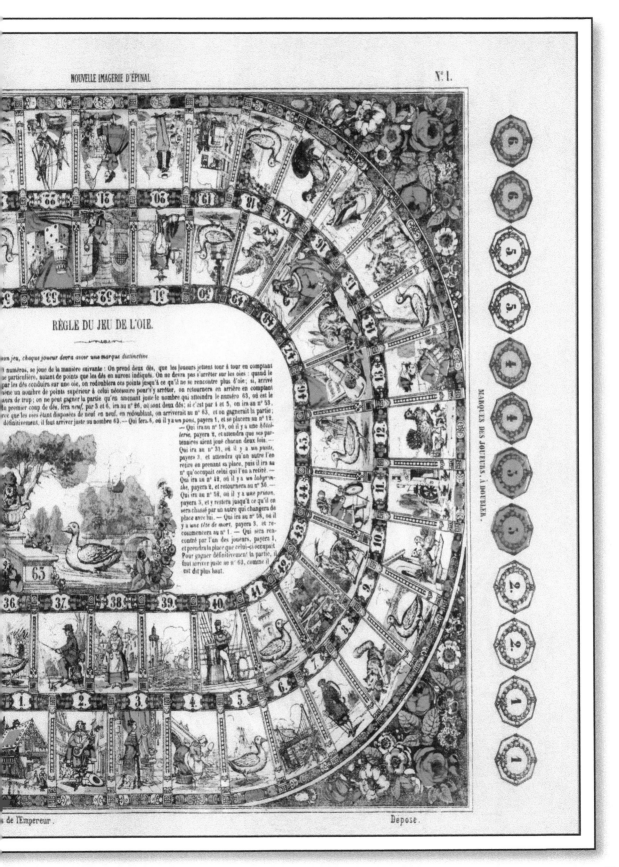

RÈGLE DU JEU DE L'OIE.

ron jeu, chaque joueur devra avoir une marque distinctive

3 numéros, se joue de la manière suivante : On prend deux dés, que les joueurs jettent tour à tour en comptant
e particulière, autant de points que les dés en auront indiqués. On ne devra pas s'arrêter sur les oies : quand le
par les dés conduira sur une oie, on redoublera ces points jusqu'à ce qu'il ne se rencontre plus d'oie ; si, arrivé
ene un nombre de points supérieur à celui nécessaire pour s'arrêter, on retournera en arrière en comptant
aura de trop ; on ne peut gagner la partie qu'en amenant juste le nombre qui atteindre le numéro 63, où est le
du premier coup de dés, fera *neuf*, par 3 et 6, ira au n° 26, où sont deux dés; si c'est par 4 et 5, on ira au n° 53,
rce que les oies étant disposées de neuf en neuf, en redoublant, on arriverait au n° 63, et on gagnerait la partie;
définitivement, il faut arriver juste au nombre 63. — Qui fera 6, où il y a un *pons*, payera 1, et se placera au n° 12.
— Qui ira au n° 19, où il y a une *hôtel-
lerie*, payera 2, et attendra que ses par-
tenaires aient joué chacun deux fois. —
Qui ira au n° 31, où il y a un *puits*,
payera 3, et attendra qu'un autre l'en
retire en prenant sa place, puis il ira au
n° qu'occupait celui qui l'en a retiré. —
Qui ira au n° 42, où il y a un *labyrin-
the*, payera 2, et retournera au n° 30. —
Qui ira au n° 52, où il y a une *prison*,
payera 3, et y restera jusqu'à ce qu'il en
sera chassé par un autre qui changera de
place avec lui. — Qui ira au n° 58, où il
y a une *tête de mort*, payera 3, et re-
commencera au n° 1. — Qui sera rencontré par l'un des joueurs, payera 1,
et prendra la place que celui-ci occupait
Pour gagner définitivement la partie, il
faut arriver juste au n° 63, comme il
est dit plus haut.

MARQUES DES JOUEURS, À DOUBLER.

THE ROYAL GAME OF G

16

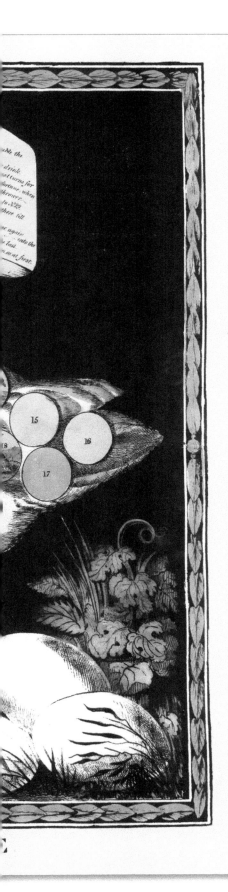

Games fashioned after a goose emerged at the century's onset. This particular version, credited to Edward Wallis of London (as noted in the minuscule text on one of the eggs), hails from around 1840. This was a period when the Game of the Goose's allure was waning in England. The dominant goose imagery undeniably grabs attention, but the game remains largely true to its classic roots. A notable variation is the absence of the first two geese on the track, a common modification in English Goose games. This adjustment eliminates the need for a unique rule governing an initial dice roll of nine, thereby removing the possibility of a swift victory. Perhaps the austere English mindset deemed such a quick win unsporting, leading to the removal of these geese. The game's guidelines specify that each participant should possess twelve counters termed 'for fish.' This terminology likely derives from a misinterpretation of the French word *fiches*, which refers to counters used as stakes in gaming. In England, counters often adopted a fish-like shape, playfully nodding to this linguistic pun.

Game of the Goose.
Milan: Eliseo Macchi
about 1900

Certain Game of the Goose variations expand the traditional 63-space layout to encompass 90 spaces. This modification traces its origins to Italy, where the number 90 holds a special allure. This fondness for the number is due to its association with the Italian State Lottery, which draws from 90 balls. One early outcome of the Italian unification in the 1860s was the consolidation of regional lotteries, triggering a nationwide gambling frenzy. Ever cautious, game manufacturers included a stipulation that, by mutual agreement, participants could opt to play using the conventional endpoint at space 63. Adapting the goose-themed spaces, spaced by nine, to fit the extended layout posed no challenge. However, the introduction of new obstacles became necessary: notably, the *fountain* at space 71, which serves as an obstruction, and the *tower* at space 82, governed by rules akin to those of the *prison*.

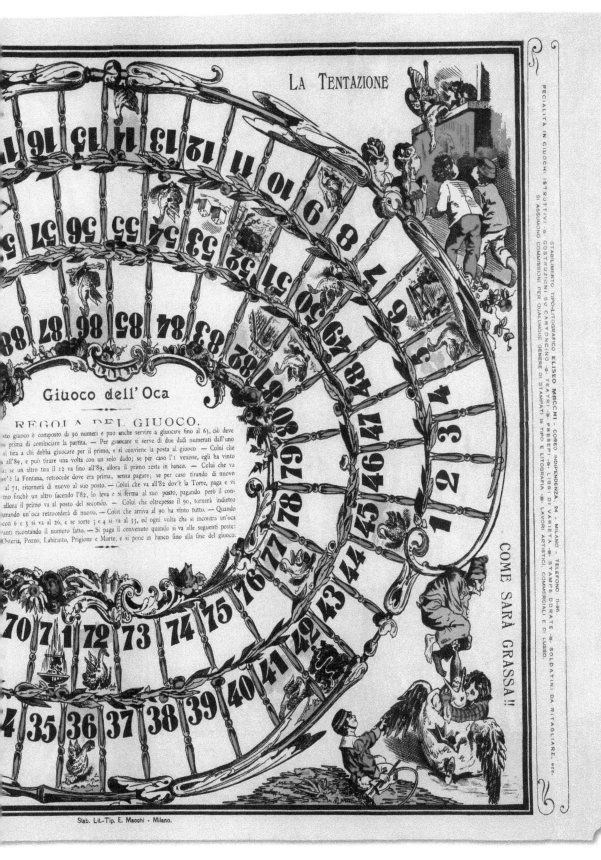

La Tentazione

Giuoco dell'Oca

REGOLA DEL GIUOCO.

...sto giuoco è composto di 90 numeri e può anche servire a giuocare fino a 63, ciò deve
...si prima di cominciare la partita. — Per giuocare si serve di due dadi numerati dall'uno
...si tira a chi debba giuocare per il primo, e si conviene la posta al giuoco — Colui che
...all'89, e può tirare una volta con un solo dado; se per caso l'1 venisse, egli ha vinto
...; se un altro tira il 12 va fino all'89, allora il primo resta in banco. — Colui che va
...ov'è la Fontana, retrocede dove era prima, senza pagare; se per caso tirando di nuovo
...al 71, ritornerà di nuovo al suo posto. — Colui che va all'82 dov'è la Torre, paga e vi
...mo finché un altro facendo l'82, lo leva e si ferma al suo posto, pagando però il con-
...allora il primo va al posto del secondo. — Colui che oltrepassa il 90, tornerà indietro
...trando un'oca retrocederà di nuovo. — Colui che arriva al 90 ha vinto tutto. — Quando
...con 6 e 3 si va al 26, e se sorte 5 e 4 si va al 53, ed ogni volta che si incontra un'oca
...anti ricontando il numero fatto. — Si paga il convenuto quando si va alle seguenti poste:
...Osteria, Pozzo, Labirinto, Prigione e Morte, e si pone in banco fino alla fine del giuoco.

COME SARÀ GRASSA!!

STABILIMENTO TIPO-LITOGRAFICO ELISEO MACCHI - CORSO INDIPENDENZA, 24 - MILANO - TELEFONO 11-96.
PECIALITÀ IN GIUOCHI ISTRUTTIVI E COSTRUZIONI SU CARTONCINO • TEATRI • PRESEPI • LIBRI DI VARIETÀ • STAMPE DONATE • SOLDATINI DA RITAGLIARE, ecc.
SI ASSUMONO COMMISSIONI PER QUALUNQUE GENERE DI STAMPATI IN TIPO E LITOGRAFIA • LAVORI ARTISTICI, COMMERCIALI E DI LUSSO.

Stab. Lit.-Tip. E. Macchi - Milano.

New Improved Goose Game. Nuremberg: Campe about 1820

German variations of the Game of the Goose from the 19th century exhibited remarkable deviations from the classic design, introducing a range of rule changes. One such variant, *The New Improved Goose Game*, retains the traditional 63 spaces but incorporates distinctive alterations, including alternative depictions for several of the established obstacles. A notable feature of this game is the depiction of geese facing either in the direction of the game's progression or against it. As delineated in the provided rules, geese facing forward serve their typical role, allowing players to double their dice throw, while those oriented backward halt players in their tracks. Interestingly, this specific rule appears exclusive to German versions. However, in the Netherlands, players often adopt a similar rule, deciding upon it by mutual agreement, even though it isn't formally documented.

Neues verbessertes Gänse-Spiel.

(Regeln.) Dieses Spiel wird mit zwei Würfeln gespielt. Jeder Spieler setzt 12 Marken in die Casse № 63. Wer mit dem ersten Wurf 5 und 4 wirft, geht sogleich auf № 53, worauf er ein beliebiges Zeichen setzt, wirft er 6 und 3 so kömt er auf № 26. Wer 6 wirft zahlt 3 Marken in die Casse und kömt auf № 12. Wer auf № 61 kömt, muss so lange warten, bis die übrigen Spieler zweimal geworfen haben. Wer auf № 31 kömt, setzt so lange aus, bis einer der Mitspieler gleiche Nummer trifft und nimt dann dessen früheren Platz ein. Wer auf № 42 kommt zahlt 3 Marken und geht auf № 30 zurück. Wer auf № 52 kömt, zahlt 3 Marken und nuss das Spiel von Vornen beginnen. Wer auf eine rückwärts gehende Gans zu stehen kömt, zahlt 3 Marken u. geht um das doppelte seines Wurfes zurück, wer hingegen auf eine vorwärts stehende Gans kömt, dessen Wurf zahlt doppelt und geht er um so viel weiter. Wer endlich auf № 63 kömt, hat das Spiel, mit dem darin befindlichen Einsätze gewonnen.

№ 844.　　　　　　　　　　　　　　　　　　　　Nürnberg bei Fr. Nap. Campe.

Game of the Monkeys. Metz: Delhalt

about 1880

A popular way to update the Goose game was to replace the geese
with monkeys. This wasn't a new concept: in fact, a game with this exact
substitution was printed in Italy as early as 1588, around the same time as
the first printed Games of the Goose. The fascination in art for portraying
monkeys as caricatures of humans (*singerie*) has been prominent in
various eras, but the 19th century saw a surge of such depictions, and
printed games picked up on this trend. Occasionally, the monkey games
were direct replacements in the traditional Game of the Goose, such as in
the *Game of the Monkeys*, produced in Metz in the northeast of France.
The primary attraction here is the humorous depictions of monkeys on the
track, all engaging in very human-like activities: smoking, taking a fancy
stroll, or trying (and failing) to catch a butterfly. However, the illustrations
outside the track are equally intriguing, especially the two monkeys at the
bottom, fervently competing in a game of dice.

The New Game of the Monkey. London: Wallis 1820

Our second monkey game is from England. At first glance, *The New Game of the Monkey* appears to be a standard 63-space Goose game with monkeys in place of geese. However, there are notable differences. Rather than the usual doubling of the throw, specific rules are assigned to each monkey space. For instance, the *Dancing Monkeys* require a player to pay one stake for dance lessons, the *Soldier* can march to No. 13, and the *Dandy* has to pay two stakes for his silliness. Nonetheless, the hazard spaces closely resemble those in the Goose game and occupy the same positions. For instance, at the *Bridge, you* have to pay a stake for the Toll; at the *Inn*, you must skip a turn and have a drink; if you land on the *Well*, you have to wait until another player comes to help you out. The 58th space, showcasing the despondent *Gamester*, mirrors the death space, meaning you have to start over.

The corner decorations are amusing, even though they're unrelated to the game's mechanics. One depicts a judge puzzled by a red herring, with a book titled 'Black...' (likely referring to Blackstone's *Commentaries on the Laws of England*) on the floor nearby. The opposite corner features two monkeys punishing a dog tethered to a pot. Above, a monkey gazes at its reflection in a mirror. Meanwhile, in the last corner, a monkey is ensnared in a steel trap — a potential reference to the anti-slavery movement? The 'lady' being wooed at space 14 sports a pot as a hat, reminiscent of Tenniel's depiction of Tweedledum in Lewis Carroll's later work, *Through the Looking-Glass*. The monkey at space 23 dons attire akin to Little Red Riding Hood, while the one at space 18 has a bellows for a hat. Truly, a delightful touch of English eccentricity!

RULES.

1st. This Game is played with a Totetum and any number of persons may play at it.

2nd. Whatever number is spun the player must place his counter under that No. and at every spin add the No. he turns up to his former one.

Whoever spins 5 must pay one for learning to Dance.

He that spins 6 must pay one for Toll.

He that comes to the Totetum may spin again.

The Soldier, No 9 may march to No 13.

Courtship, No 14 may go to the Inn No 19.

Whoever comes to The Inn No 19 must stop a turn & Drink.

Whoever falls into The Well No 31 must stop there till some one comes to the same No and helps him out.

He that gets into The Maze, No 42 must begin again.

Whoever gets into Prison, No 52 must stop there 3 turns.

The Gamester, No 58 must begin again.

The Dandy, No 59 must pay two for his folly.

He that comes exactly to 63 wins The Game, but whoever goes beyond it must go back to No 50.

When two come to the same No the last must go back to his former place.

Published by E. Wallis, 42 Skinner Street, Snow Hill, London

25

London:Published by William Spooner 379 Strand Nov.r 5.th

26

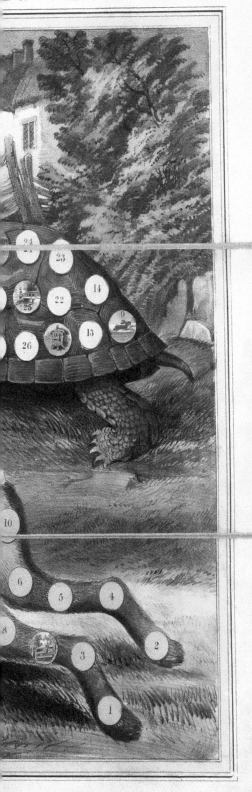

The Hare and the Tortoise.
London: Spooner
1859

Other animals were used to refresh the Game of the Goose. The Hare and the Tortoise, released in London in 1859 as a stunning color lithograph, offers an innovative twist by splitting the game's path between a magnificent illustration of the tortoise and an even grander depiction of the hare. The game starts at the hare's back left foot, snakes between its hind legs up to space 8 — but you'll find space 9 on the tortoise. After that, the path returns to the hare before branching out once more. Some spaces feature a small image of a hare; here, the player has to skip a turn and contribute two counters to the pool. On spaces showcasing a tortoise, the player doubles their throw, similar to the Game of the Goose. Many spaces located on the tortoise reward the player with three counters. Additionally, there are hazard spaces that echo the Game of the Goose. This game, like its predecessor, spans 63 spaces in length. Players need to stay sharp when moving their markers: if someone places theirs on the wrong number, they owe two counters to the pool.

New Game of the Hare.
Weissenberg: G Burkhardt's successors
late 19th century

Hunting has always been a cherished activity among Germans, and the *New Game of the Hare* brings this passion to the table. It's a straightforward game, played with two dice, yet the rules aren't immediately clear from the images. For instance, spaces 34, 45, 58, and 64, all showcasing a hare, serve as obstacles, sending you back to the position from which you rolled. However, not all spaces featuring a hare have this consequence. In the author's version of the game, a prior owner has marked these challenging spaces with an 'X' to help recall the rules. Space 57, which depicts a puzzled hunter who's seemingly lost track of the hare, mandates that the player begin anew.

Dieses Spiel wird mit zwei Würfeln gespielt und jeder Spieler versieht sich mit einem anderen Zeichen, um die geworfene Nummer zu besetzen. Jeder Spieler setzt 6 Marken in die Kasse. Wer beim Anspielen 1 und 6 wirft, erhält 3 Marken aus der Kasse und geht auf Nr. 12. Wirft man beim Anspielen 1 und 2, so setzt man sein Zeichen auf Nr. 26. Wirft man beim Anspielen 12, so zahlt man 6 Marken in die Kasse. Auf Nr. 19 zahlt man 4 Marken in die Kasse. Wer auf die Hasen 34, 45, 58 und 64 kommt, zahlt 2 Marken und geht auf seinen letzten Platz zurück. Auf Nr. 57 bezahlt der Spieler 3 Marken in die Kasse und fängt von vorne an zu spielen. Auf Nr. 60 muß man sitzen bleiben bis jeder Spieler 3 Mal gewürfelt hat. Wer auf 67 kommt, darf nicht mehr mitspielen. Würfe über Nr. 73 hinaus werden zurückgezählt. Wer auf Nr. 73 kommt, hat das Spiel gewonnen.

Druck und Verlag von C. Burckardt's Nachfolger in Weißenburg (Elsaß).

The Game of the Owl: and Other Lotteries

In the Game of the Owl, players placed bets into a pool, or drew from it based on the dice roll – roll sixes, and you claim the pool. Simple gambling games like this were themed in various ways.

This chapter delves into 'lottery' games of different types. Some are 'pool' games, played with dice where bets are added to or taken from a pot, which eventually goes to the victor. One of the oldest forms is the Game of the Owl. It's entirely distinct from the race games from the previous chapter, even though it's often inaccurately labeled as a Game of the Goose variant. In reality, it's debatable if it's even a board game. Although there's a game sheet, there aren't any playing pieces, and the sheet basically provides instructions on when to add to or subtract from the winner's pool. Versions exist for both two dice and three dice, but all display every possible dice combination, ensuring each roll has a clear directive on how many bets to add to or subtract from the 'pot.' In numerous game variations, the conclusion comes when a player rolls all sixes – thereby claiming everything in the pot. Some game versions are stricter. Here, each player continues until they (typically a 'he') run out of funds. When all but one have backed out, the last player standing claims the pot. Like the Game of the Goose, the Game of the Owl's principles could be reshaped to fit new themes.

The most ancient known version of the game is a unique print created in the Montorgueil area of Paris in the early 17th century, now housed in the Bibliothèque nationale de France. Yet, the game's probably even older: its title comes from the German folklore about Till Eulenspiegel, recognized in print from the early 16th century but perhaps even a century older. Till, from Brunswick, traveled Europe, pulling pranks and highlighting people's vices, and the game sheets often illustrate some of his notable antics.

Another type of lottery game is the German Game of Seven, dated around 1600. It's always played with a pair of dice. The game board functions as a betting layout, with spaces numbered from two to twelve, the seventh space centralized and others encircling it. The rules are straightforward. You sum the numbers on the dice to get your roll. For any roll excluding two (double one), twelve (double six), or seven, you place a coin on the corresponding number on the game sheet, given that space is vacant. If not, you collect the coin. Roll a seven, and you add a coin to the center space, where stakes can accumulate indefinitely. Roll a two, and you collect all coins on numbers encircling the center. Roll a twelve, and you collect all coins, including those in the center space. This game, too, can be adapted to various themes, the most controversial being the Game of the Jew, showcasing a stereotyped image of a Jewish person counting money in the center.

Both the Game of the Owl and the Game of Seven started as pure gambling games, typically associated with taverns' rough crowd. But by the 19th century, sanitized versions with harmless imagery became popular in more refined settings.

A third type of lottery game is based on the Giuoco Romano [Roman Game] or Biribissi, known in Italy since the 16th century. In this, players draw small card images from a bag or hat in turns. A game board, featuring matching images, serves as a betting layout. A banker collects and pays out at fixed rates. Often, a thick card sheet is used, displaying two sets of identical images. One set gets cut out and mixed in the bag, while the other remains intact as the betting layout. Another version uses a sheet with a single image set to be cut out and drawn from the bag. In this variant, each image instructs how much to add to or subtract from the pool, much like in the Game of the Owl. By the 19th century, this became a beloved game for kids.

Game of the Owl. Turnhout: Brepols

about 1845

This Belgian version of the *Game of the Owl* uses three dice, and every potential dice roll combination is depicted on the board, each accompanied by specific instructions. If a 'B' appears (derived from the Flemish word *betaal*, meaning 'pay'), then players are required to pay the indicated number of stakes to the pool. Conversely, if there's a 'T' (from the Flemish word *trek*, meaning 'draw'), the specified number of stakes must be drawn from the pool. The optimal rolls are when all three dice display the same number. Such rolls entitle the player to half the pool, with the exception of a triple six roll, which allows the player to claim the entire pool, resetting the game thereafter.

This game pays tribute to the tales of Eulenspiegel (translated from German as 'owl-glass,' with 'glass' referring to a mirror), as evidenced by the central image of an owl beside a mirror. This iteration, however, has been made more family-friendly for the 19th-century audience, ensuring all images are harmless. Some illustrations are notably clever; for instance, a roll of 6,6,1 reveals an image of soap bubbles accompanied by the instruction *niet* (indicating no action is needed, neither pay nor draw).

Uitlegging.

Ten 1. Zal men bespreken wat ieder zal inleggen om te beginnen en dan werpen wie eerst spelen zal; die de hoogste oogen werpt, speelt eerst, en voorts met de zon om.

» 2. Geworpen hebbende, zoekt uw getal, en is 't eene B, zoo betaalt, en is 't eene T, zoo trekt volgens de getallen.

» 3. Wie drie gelijken werpt trekt den halven Pot, doch de oneffen penning blijft bij 't spel.

» 4. Wie drie zessen werpt, trekt den geheelen Pot, en dan moet elk wederom insetten om te beginnen.

» 5. Die werpt daar NIET staat, zal voor dien tijd niets trekken.

Explication.

1. On conviendra d'abord de l'enjeu, puis on jettera les dés pour savoir qui jouera le premier; ce sera celui qui amènera le plus de points et ainsi de suite selon le cours du soleil.

2. Les dés jetés, on cherche son point. Si c'est un B, on paie, si, au contraire, c'est un T on retire du jeu une somme égale à celle que le chiffre indique.

3. Quiconque amènera trois points égaux, gagnera la moitié de la poule, mais le denier impair reste acquis au jeu.

4. Quiconque amènera les trois six, gagne la poule entière, et tous les joueurs doivent faire une nouvelle mise avant de pouvoir recommencer.

5. Quiconque tombera sur le point où se trouve le mot NIET, ne touche rien de cette fois.

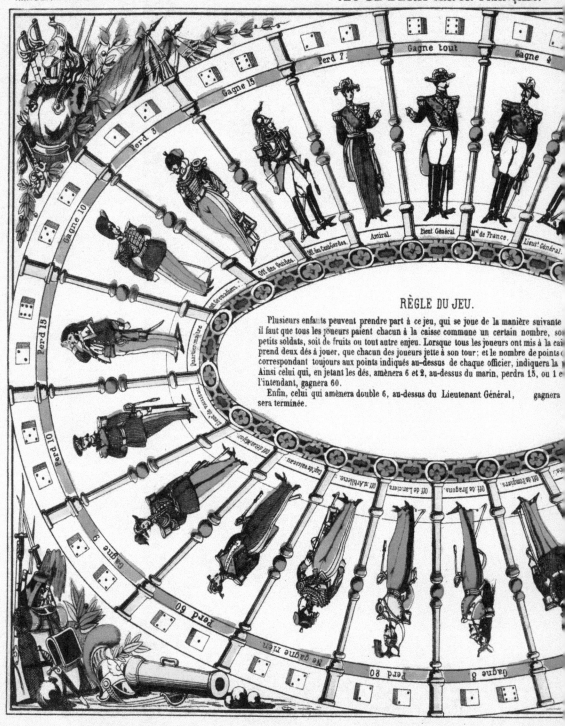

Game of the French General Military Staff. Épinal: Pellerin about 1880

The *Game of the French Miltary Staff* is a The Game of the French Military Staff is a French spin on the *Game of the Owl*, showcasing officers from the French armed forces. Players use two dice, with each potential outcome tied to a specific officer. The winning toss of a double six is linked to the Lieutenant-General — in a previous version, this was attributed to Napoleon III. It might strike some as odd that The Marshal of France isn't linked with the winning roll. However, in the 19th century, this role was more of an honorary title than a designation for the head of the French military. The game's instructions clarify its intended audience: children. They're encouraged to play for 'pictures, toy soldiers, fruits, or other stakes' — a clear sign that this once tavern game had been refined for more genteel settings. This game was a creation of the renowned Pellerin firm in Épinal, famed for their *Images d'Épinal*. Throughout the 19th century, their affordable stencil-colored woodcuts — featuring military themes, story characters, religious scenes, and card-based toys (among other topics) — found audiences not only in France but also internationally. The company continues to operate to this day.

Game of the Ship. Milan: Tamburini

about 1860

The Italian *Gioco della Barca* (Game of the Ship) is a rendition of the *Game of Seven*, played similarly with two dice. The rules, provided in Italian on the game sheet, mirror those of the *Game of Seven* detailed earlier in this chapter, meaning stakes accumulate on the central ship whenever a seven is rolled. This Milanese version from the early 1800s features meticulous hand coloring by brush, contrasting the stencil coloring typical of later mass production. The striking woodcut image of the ship, adorned with cannons, is paired with typed rules framed within an ornate border. This method offered a cost-effective way to produce a mid-tier quality print, as opposed to the pricier engraving of copper plates favored by high-end printers.

IL VERO GIUOCO DELLA BARCA

DICHIARAZIONE SOPRA IL GIUOCO DELLA BARCA.

Al Giuoco della Barca si pigliano due dadi disegnati da tutte le parti: poi si fa chi prima debba tirare, quindi s'incomincia.

I. Chi fa 3. 4. 5. 6. 8. 9. 10. 11. metterà sopra i detti numeri una moneta, e se nei suddetti numeri vi è qualche moneta si leva.

II. Chi fa 7. metterà sempre una moneta in Barca.

III. Chi fa 2. leverà tutte le monete che si trovano sopra i numeri all'intorno.

IV. Chi fa 12. leverà tutte le monete che si trovano sopra i numeri ed anche quelli che si trovano nella Barca.

Si vende in Milano nella Stamperia di Gio. Tamburini in contrada di S. Raffaele.

Turnhout — Brepols & Dierckx zoon.

38

Game of Harlequin. Turnhout: Brepols

late 19th century

The *Game of Seven* is recognized under numerous names, each carrying its own distinctive imagery. *The Game of Harlequin* might appear harmless, but its gameplay suggests otherwise. In this variation, special rules for rolling a two or twelve are omitted, treating them as regular numbers, which extends the game's duration. A roll of seven prompts money to amass on the central Harlequin figure. However, gameplay continues until only one player remains financially afloat, who then claims the entire pot. A unique rule stipulates that once a player goes broke, they're granted a final complimentary roll before their exit.

*Drink, Hansel, Drink! Germany: publisher unknown
about 1900*

*S*chluck Hänsel, Schluck! [Drink, Hansel, Drink! – the title is clarified on a
separate rule sheet] presents a comedic twist on the *Game of Seven*, showcasing
a vivid chromolithographed board. This inclusion in a collection of German games
from the late 1800s allegedly originates 'in upper Bavaria or the Austrian Alps,'
though this claim lacks concrete proof. Just as in the prior game, the 'last man
standing' claims victory. However, this version limits each player to four counters,
leveling the playing field for children. The board's vibrant illustrations likely draw
from German folklore.

41

Game of the Pedlar. England: publisher unknown

late 19th century

'Central seven' games didn't gain much traction in England, though an iteration known as the *Game of the Jew* did emerge in the early 1800s. The *Game of the Pedlar* stands out as a unique variant. While its rules align closely with the *Game of the Ship*, a roll of double ones isn't specially treated. Players can use two dice or a twelve-sided teetotum. However, oversight occurs if the teetotum lands on one, as the game sheet doesn't recognize this number!

THE GAME OF THE PEDLAR.

2	7	6
3		8
4		9
5	11	10

DIRECTIONS.

This Game is played either with a pair of Dice or Teetotum marked with 12 sides & any number of persons can play. In order to decide who shall begin the game, each person throws & the highest number plays first; & the number thrown he must cover with a counter the corresponding one on the Board, each in their turn doing the same provided it is uncovered; if it is already covered, he claims the counter on that particular number: exception is taken to Nº 7; any one throwing that number pays to The Pedlar, which remains until one of the party throws 12 and he clears the Board, including The Pedlar, and the game recommences.

Game of the Apple – New Zanzibar.
France: publisher unknown
late 19th century

Up next is a seldom-seen French adaptation of the 'central seven' model, intriguingly titled: *Game of the Apple – New Zanzibar*. In late 1800s France, 'Zanzibar' was slang for a three-dice gambling game. Rolling three matching numbers would elicit a 'Zanzi!' cheer from the victor, though the reason for this remains unknown. The game's apple connection also remains a mystery. This particular printed version relies on two dice and sticks to the conventional Game of Seven rules.

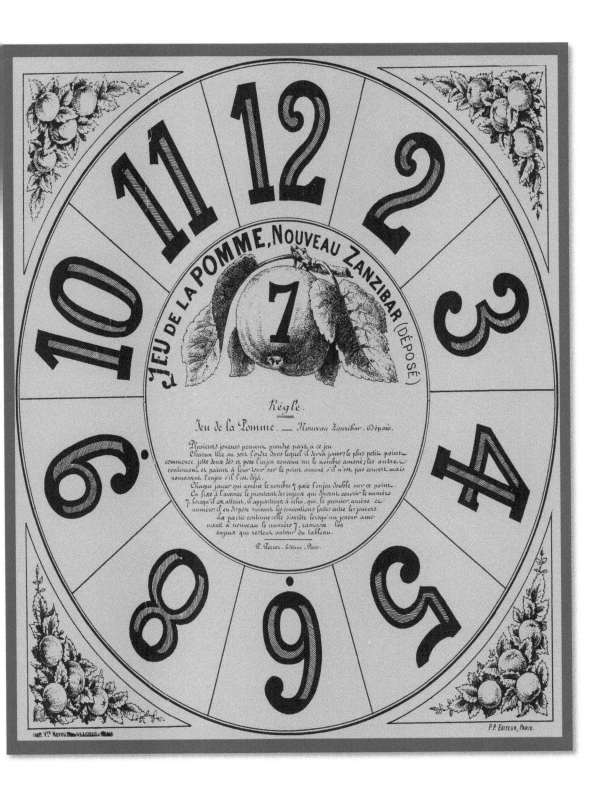

Game of the Omnibus and White Ladies.
France: publisher unknown
about 1830

*J*eu des omnibus et dames blanches [Game of the Omnibus and White
Ladies] diverges in gameplay. Its exquisite central illustration depicts a
stylish group of men and women engrossed in play. Surrounding them are
images of various horse-drawn omnibuses, numbered 1 through 12, where
bets are placed. Players draw wooden balls, also numbered 1-12, from a
bag to determine winning numbers. The game's guidelines state: 'In this
game, one discovers one's true nature: the adept player remains composed.'
Yet, one depicted player appears to be in sheer distress! Dating back to
the 1830s, this game draws its title from *les Dames blanches*, one of the
omnibus lines introduced in Paris during that era. Its elegance inspired the
design for the debut Hermès scarf, which, while still in production, now
boasts fresh color schemes.

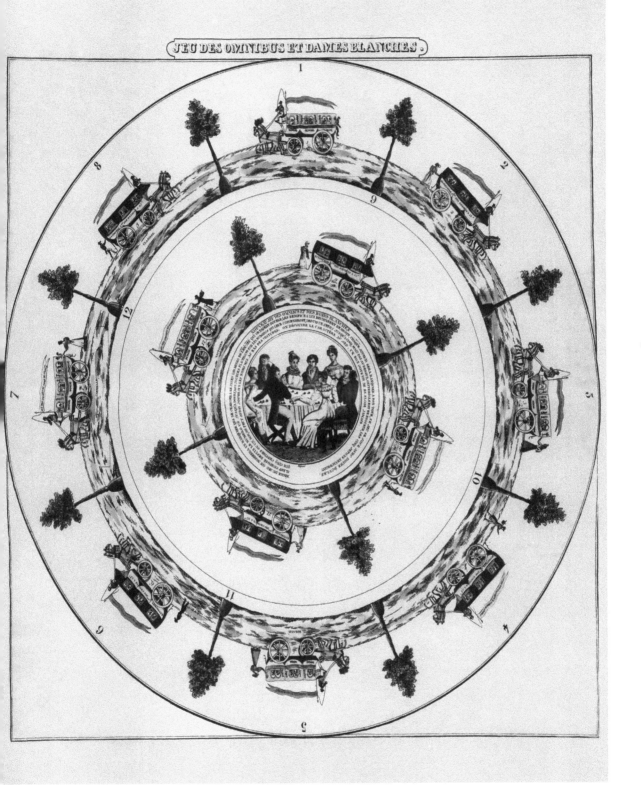

NUEVA LOTERÍA PARA NIÑOS.

(Núm. 74.)

La fortuna, todo lo gana. — La esgrima, ni gana ni pierde. — La equitacion, gana 2. — La gimnasia, gana 4. — La limosna, gana 10. — La devocion gana 8.

El baile, ni gana ni pierde. — El colegial, gana 2. — El cadete, gana 3. — El aprendiz, gana 1. — El escribiente gana 2. — La lectura, gana 8.

El granuja, pierde 5. — El holgazan, pierde 4. — El miedoso, pierde 1. — El monaguillo, gana 3. — El corneta, pierde 2. — El tambor, pierde 4.

El postillon, gana 8. — El pastor, ni gana ni pierde. — El lazarillo, gana 2. — El burlon, pierde 5. — El goloso, pierde 3. — El pollo, pierde 5.

El grumete, pierde 7. — El desobediente, pierde 10. — El pillete, pierde 12. — El camorrista, pierde 6. — El barquillero, pierde 4. — El arenero, pierde 2.

El limpia botas, gana 5. — El organillo, gana 2. — El lacayo, gana 4. — El fosforero, gana 3. — El hortera, gana 8. — Los niños premiados, gana 4.

El travieso, pierde 12. — El columpio, pierde 1. — Saca el rabo, pierde 6. — Pasatiempo, ni gana ni pierde. — El compasivo, gana 20. — Cariño fraternal, gana 4.

Donde las dan las toman, p. 9. — La pedrea, pierde 8. — El premio, gana 12. — El castigo, pierde 6. — El enfermo, pierde 14. — La muerte, todo lo pierde.

EXPLICACION DEL MODO QUE SE HA DE JUGAR.—Se recortan las 48 aleluyas de este pliego, y, arrolladas, se colocan dentro de una gorra ó bolsa. Se forma un depósito de aleluyas, ó lo que se quiera jugar, por partes iguales, entre los que juegan. Cada jugador, por turno, saca una aleluya de la bolsa; si le toca una de ganar toma del fondo tantas como dice el letrero; si la saca de perder, pone las que marca la misma. Si saca la muerte, pierde tantas como haya en el depósito; y si saca la fortuna, gana todo lo del fondo, y concluye la partida, volviendo á empezar de nuevo.

MADRID.—Despacho calle de Juanelo, núm. 19

48

New Lottery for Children. Madrid: Despacho about 1880

Shifting gears, the next game functions as a lottery where winning and losing chances are plucked from a bag. The *Nueva Loteria per Ninos* [New Lottery for Children], a straightforward print from Madrid, depicts relatable everyday scenes for children. Intended to be sectioned into 48 individual scenes, each piece was rolled and stowed in a bag. Players would draw scenes sequentially, each accompanied by instructions on stakes to deposit or withdraw from the pot. For instance, the final row describes various situations, from tit-for-tat scenarios to depictions of illness and even death. The game concludes when the cornucopia, the first scene, is drawn, allowing the drawer to claim the remaining pot. This game sheet offers a keen glimpse into life in Spain during the late 1800s.

Educational Games: Learning for Pleasure?

First appearing in France in the seventeenth century, educational games based on the *Game of the Goose* remained popular two hundred years later and were enjoyable to play. However, the English games of the nineteenth century, while showcasing stunning images, often included detailed instruction booklets with lengthy passages to read aloud, resulting in a slow-paced and tedious game.

Perhaps the inaugural educational board game was the Jeu du monde [Game of the World] crafted by the map-maker Pierre Duval in 1645. It featured a spiral track of vignette maps representing various countries. Its nod to the Game of the Goose was evident, with the track spanning 63 spaces and the winning position symbolizing France.

History-teaching games also originated in mid-seventeenth-century France. Typically, historical events are chronologically arranged along a spiral track. This strict sequence offers *limited flexibility to game designers, meaning these games often vary in track length and don't closely relate to the Game of the Goose.*

England caught on to the trend of educational games later. The earliest known example is a mid-eighteenth-century map game centered on the Grand Tour of Europe – a rite of passage for affluent young Englishmen. Unlike French geography games, this map presented a zigzag of numbered locations. Titled the Journey through Europe and crafted by John Jefferys, the game had unique rules. The capital cities, described as 'where a king resides,' functioned like Goose spaces, doubling the player's move. However, by the nineteenth century, ties to the Game of the Goose had mostly faded in newer games.

The Georgian era marked a golden period for educational games in England. Philosopher John Locke (1632-1704) shared his educational perspectives in 'Some Thoughts Concerning Education' (1693), a guide for grooming young gentlemen. Locke believed in integrating play into education. He commented, 'None of the topics they are to study should ever become a burden to them.'

This philosophy birthed the concept of learning through play. English game manufacturers swiftly catered to the burgeoning middle class of the Industrial Revolution. However, these games bore a weighty intent. They were accompanied by pamphlets elaborating on the geographical locations or historical events in the game. For children, these extensive readings were dull. Moreover, the unpredictable sequence, a hallmark of dice or teetotum games, impeded systematic learning.

By the Victorian period, educators began doubting the efficacy of game-based learning. Consequently, game themes started mirroring leisure activities rather than adhering to a stringent educational curriculum – a trend mirrored in France.

In the Netherlands, where the Game of the Goose retained its charm, educational games for younger kids emerged as early as the eighteenth century, notably the ABC games. The nineteenth century in this region witnessed not only serious instructional games but also delightful ones with playful elements, like the one described in this chapter, which narrates the tale of the renowned Dutch Admiral, Michael de Ruyter.

In conclusion, the ingenuity of educational game designers is impressive. They often ingeniously blended innovative concepts with the foundational structures of age-old games. The allure of later games, enriched with vibrant colors, can be attributed to advancements in printing technologies, making these games often humorous and sharp-witted.

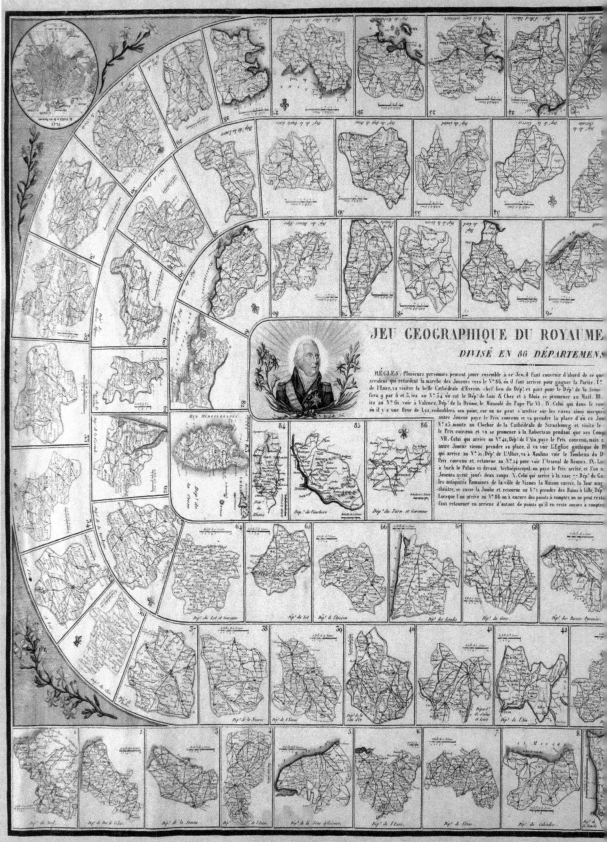

JEU GEOGRAPHIQUE DU ROYAUME
DIVISÉ EN 86 DÉPARTEMENS

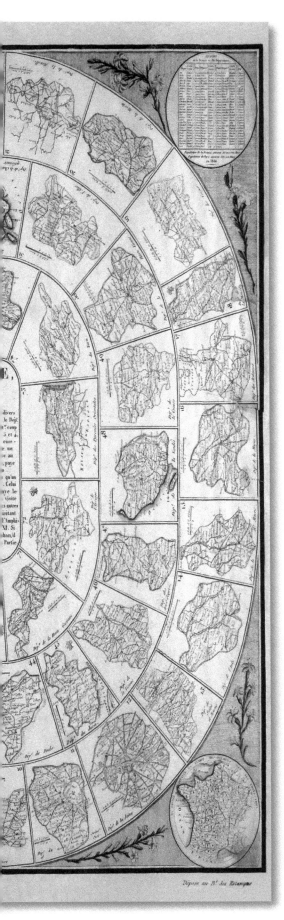

Dépose au B.l des Estampes

Geographical Game
of the Kingdom of France.
Paris: Basset

1816

This is a direct descendant of Duval's *Game of the World*. Here, though, its spiral track consists of small maps of the Departments of France, which had replaced the old Provinces after the French Revolution of 1789. The first version of this map game appeared under the title *Geographical Game of the Republic of France* around 1795. The version shown here is a later edition, produced around 1816 to recognize the restoration of the Bourbon monarchy. A portrait of Louis XVIII now graces the game, and its title has changed to *Geographical Game of the Kingdom of France*. In nineteenth-century France, producers of printed games had to be agile to keep up with regime changes. The game is clearly derived from the Game of the Goose: certain spaces are marked with a tiny *fleur-de-lys*, the badge of French royalty, to denote throw-doubling spaces, similar to those marked with a goose in the original game. In the initial version, these spaces were marked with a tiny Gallic rooster, symbolizing the Revolution. Some of the playing instructions are amusing. At space 77, the Department of Gard, the player visits Roman antiquities in Nismes [Nîmes] but trips over in the ruins of the amphitheater, breaks a leg, and has to return to space 1, the Baths at Lille.

Game of the End of the Century.
Paris: Saussine
1899

Closing this chapter and the nineteenth century on a high note, the *Jeu fin de siècle* [Game of the End of the Century] graphically celebrates the period's many accomplishments. The game commences with an infant in a cradle at space 1, representing the dawn of a new century, while the departing eighteenth century is personified by an elderly man laden with a bag filled with now-obsolete inventions, such as the semaphore. Each space on the track highlights an invention or milestone accompanied by its corresponding date, culminating at space 52 where a tombstone marks the 'demise' of the nineteenth century, signaling players to begin anew. The game's central, triumphant space teases a futuristic vision: a journey from Paris to Marseille in just five minutes aboard a magnificent flying contraption. The iconic Eiffel Tower seems minuscule next to an imposing counterpart, and an impressively long bridge spans the English Channel. Blue-numbered spaces on the track are reminiscent of the traditional 'goose' spaces, where a player's roll is doubled. The white-numbered spaces lead players through a series of challenges, compelling them to progress step by step until they can re-enter the main game, equipped with all the knowledge they've gained, at the *Expo Universelle 1889*. The game's illustrations, which showcase accurate depictions of the era's attire, underscore the meticulous effort invested to capture the essence of the period authentically.

New Historical and Chronological Game of the French Monarchy.
Paris: Basset
1810

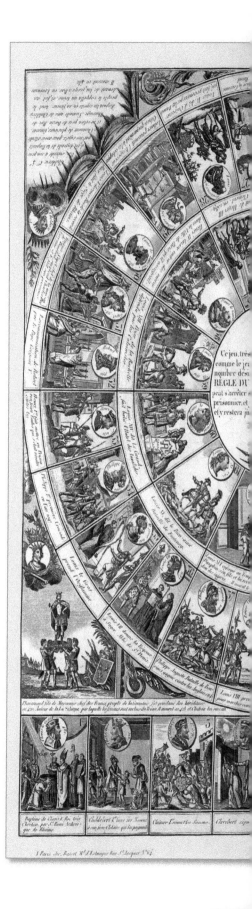

This historical game showcases the lineage of French monarchs starting with Clovis (c. 466-511), the first king to unify the Franks. Published in Paris in 1814, the game celebrates Louis XVIII's triumphant entry into Paris, depicted in the central, winning space, featuring a balloon adorned with flags – game publishers loved to stay updated with technology! The 63-space track is clearly inspired by the Game of the Goose, with several spaces marked with the royal *fleur-de-lys* for throw-doubling. The equivalent of the *death* space, unusually located at number 57, displays the assassination of Henri III by a Catholic zealot in 1589. Space 31, reminiscent of the *prison* space, portrays the capture and imprisonment by Hugues Capet (c. 939-996, king of the Franks from 987) of Charles, Duke of Lorraine, who had challenged the succession. These implicit references to the Game of the Goose were designed to make events memorable and would have been recognized by all players.

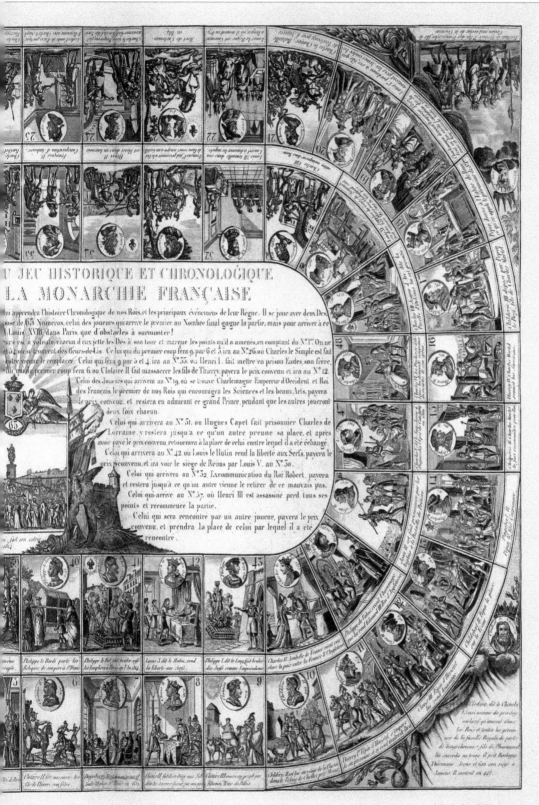

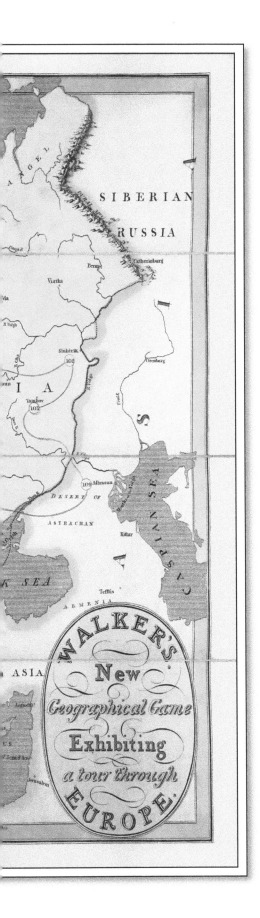

*W*alker's *New Geographical Game exhibiting a Tour through Europe,*' dated 1810, is a stark contrast, stemming instead from John Jeffery's game of the Grand Tour. The track is displayed on a large map of Europe, with numbered circles representing towns and cities visited, each described in detail in the 34-page booklet sold with the game. Some places have special instructions, though most are quite plain: e.g., 'Paris – here wait four turns to view the city.' However, the city of Nantes (space 32) seems to have elicited a sharper instruction, almost equivalent to the *death* space. 'It was here that the famous edict in favor of the Protestants was published in 1598, but in less than a century, it was revoked by the celebrated Louis XIV. Here, go back to no. 1, London.' Georgian London was firmly Protestant, but the keen irony in the word 'celebrated' is evident. This game was published by W & T Darton, and as we will see in the subsequent chapter, the Dartons were unafraid to promote their views through their games for youngsters.

Historical Pastime. London: Passmore

1847

Games teaching History were also popular in England in the nineteenth century. The earliest English example is *Historical Pastime*, published in London in 1803 by John Harris and John Wallis. It chronicles English History events from the Battle of Hastings in 1066 up to the game's publication. George III's portrait adorns the central space of the game, and each edition was updated to reflect the ruling monarch. Hence, the 1837 edition features a young Queen Victoria, with a preceding space referencing the abolition of slavery. The game sheet, meticulously hand-colored, boasts battle scenes from British victories at Seringapatam (1799), Trafalgar (1805), Waterloo (1815), and Navarino (1827), emphasizing the potency of the British military. Some spaces have specialized instructions, some of which require player participation, adding to the game's educational value. For instance, space 28 features Roger Bacon, a 13th-century English philosopher, with the instruction: 'Mention some discovery of this genius or pay one to the Treasury.'

61

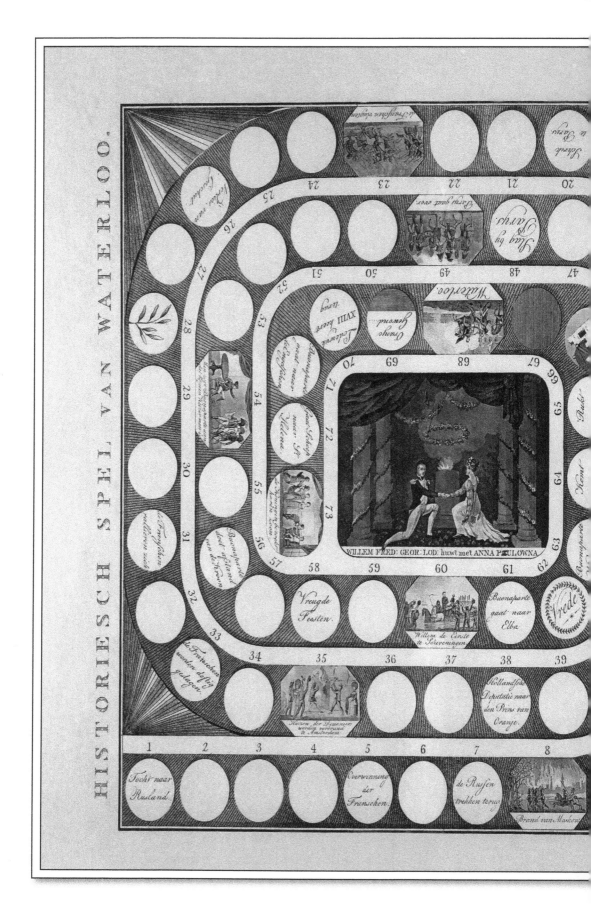

WILLEM FRED: GEOR: LOD: huwt met ANNA PAULOWNA

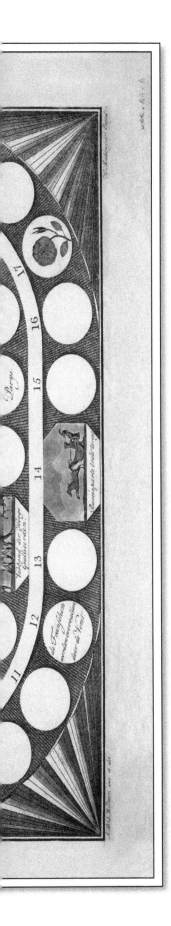

Historic Game of Waterloo.
Amsterdam: Moolenijzer
1816 / 1817

T he Battle of Waterloo also gets a nod in the *Historisch Spel van Waterloo* [Historic Game of Waterloo], published in Amsterdam in 1816/1817. This exquisite game sheet, produced using a sophisticated etching method known as aquatint, is a far cry from a 'popular print.' An accompanying explanatory booklet doesn't mince words: 'The Waterloo game aims to supplant the Goose Game, from which children learned nothing, and to engrave in the minds of Dutch youth the valiant deeds since 1812.' The central illustration, forming the final space, depicts the engagement of the Prince of Orange to Anna Pavlovna – they were wed in St. Petersburg in 1816.

De Ruyter Game.
Amsterdam: Vlieger
about 1890

Michiel de Ruyter (1607-1676), a highly skilled admiral with several victories against the French and English, including a daring raid on the Medway in 1667, is the focus of this vibrant chromolithographed game. It's a 63-space game, but its rules are unique and barely resemble the Game of the Goose. It's craftily designed for children's entertainment. Landing on space 2 requires children to sing the de Ruyter song, highlighting Michiel's younger days. His act of scaling the church tower, portrayed at space 3, necessitates the child landing there to replicate him by standing on a chair. There are special rules for the majestic row of cannons aligning the ship's broadside. The depiction of de Ruyter outdrinking his friends (space 15) might now be seen as inappropriate, but on the whole, the game effectively familiarized Dutch kids with their naval heritage in an engaging manner.

The Pleasures of Astronomy.
London: Wallis
1804

Instruction in science wasn't overlooked in the 19th century, though there are fewer examples of games for this subject than for geography and history. This exceptional English game, *The Pleasures of Astronomy*, showcases the original observatory at Greenwich, London, which defines the prime meridian, at its center. Surrounding it are portraits of Ptolemy, Tycho Brahe, Copernicus, and Sir Isaac Newton. The game was 'revised and approved by Mrs. Bryan of Blackheath.' She operated a school in London and was a trailblazer in science education for girls. The rulebook that comes with the game hints that she didn't have much patience for those not paying attention:

Space 6: *The County Gaol* — This is where you end up if you're more interested in the movements of billiard balls than the movements of planets. However tough you think you've got it, stay here until someone else takes your spot.

Space 15: *The Man in the Moon* — Some uninformed folks believe there's a Man in the Moon, with a dog and a bundle of wood, who changes its appearance by eating it away, and they say it grows back every month. To get the real scoop, go back to No. 13, [The Phases of the Moon], and read the description there for yourself.

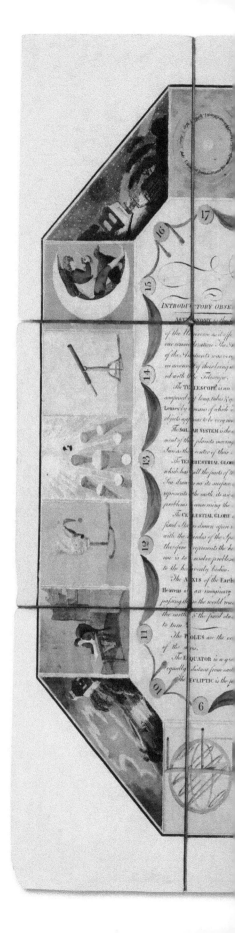

SCIENCE in SPORT, or the

PLEASURES OF ASTRONOMY;

Instructive Pastime. Revised & approved by M. Bryan, Blackheath.

LAWS of the GAME.

FLAMSTEAD HOUSE.

Published by EDWARD WALLIS, 42, Skinner Street, Snow Hill, London. _____ of whom may be had
Science in Sport or the Pleasure of NATURAL PHILOSOPHY, an Entertaining Game.

JEU DES CONTES DES FÉES

RÈGLE DU JEU.

Premièrement. Il faut convenir de ce qu'on veut jouer et de ce qu'on doit payer aux rencontres et accidents. Il est à noter que 63 nombres, et celui qui le premier atteint le nombre final, gagne la partie; mais on n'arrive pas aisément à la Reine des Fées, c'est-à-dire obstacles se présentent avant qu'on y puisse aboutir. Pour jouer à ce jeu, on prend deux dés, des que chacun pour sa jette une fois, et il y a autant

La Reine des Fées.

63

L'Aimable Migeunot. (Dans Chatte Blanche.)

Game of Fairy Tales.
Metz: Didion
late 19th century

Games were also designed to appeal to younger players. This particular game features 63 spaces teeming with fairy tale characters: the Blue Bird, the Beauty with Golden Hair, the White Cat, and many more. In this adaptation, fairies take on the role traditionally held by geese, appearing in the two-track series that begin on spaces 5 and 9, respectively. The game interprets hazard spaces with a clever touch. For instance, instead of the standard bridge at space 6, an ogress awaits, sending the player to space 12 to meet a gruesome end by an ogre. The notorious *death* space at 58 depicts a dragon feasting on a knight, signaling the player to start over. Notably, there's a humorous twist to the initial roll of 9: a magician propels the player to space 26 when rolling a 6 and 3, while seven-league boots whisk the player to space 53 upon rolling a 5 and 4. This game, a wood engraving embellished with stencil color, was economically produced, catering to the budget-conscious segment of the young market.

The Potatoes Game. Germany: publisher unknown
late 19th century

In a unique take on educational board games, this modest game introduces players to the theme of potato farming. It's presented as a straightforward, uncolored lithograph, featuring rules in both French and German – a nod to its Alsatian origins. Gameplay follows uncomplicated instructions, like paying or drawing from the pool or moving forward and backward on a concise, 25-space circular track. Among the game's directives, the one that stands out in relation to the game's imagery is at space 19: unloading the cart takes so long that the player must wait for a companion, who then swaps places with them, reminiscent of the traditional *well* or *prison* rule. The illustrations shed light on the stages of potato farming, from planting to feasting. These images are detailed, providing a clear view of the equipment in use and underscoring the delineation between tasks for men and women. At the game's heart, a depiction of a farmer's family gathered around a meal, expressing gratitude for their sustenance, provides an authentic glimpse into the humble rural life of that era.

Das Kartoffel-Spiel.

Jeder Spieler setzt 12 Marken in die Kasse und nimmt irgend eine Sache zum Setzen. Nun wird gewürfelt. Wer zuerst nach N° 3 kommt, setzt sein Zeichen auf N° 1 und fängt das Spiel an. Wirft er N° 4, so rückt er gleich weiter auf N° 15. N° 6 bezahlt 2 Marken. N° 10 bekommt 5 Marken und rückt auf N° 13. Wer 12 wirft, geht wieder auf N° 7 zurück. N° 18 bezahlt 4 Marken. Wer N° 9 wirft, bekommt 6 Marken und geht weiter auf N° 21. Wer nach N° 19 kommt, hilft so lange den Wagen, abladen bis ihn ein Anderer ablöst. In der Küche bleibt man so lange, bis man noch 3 Augen wirft, worauf man das Spiel gewonnen hat und Alles bekommt, was in der Kasse ist, und sich auf den für ihn bereit stehenden Stuhl setzt und ißt. Die Nummern 2. 5. 8. 11. 14. 17. 20. 23. zahlen alle 1 Marke Strafe. Wer über 25 wirft, geht wieder so weit zurück, als er Augen mehr hat.

Le jeu des pommes de terre.

Chaque joueur paye 12 marques dans la caisse et prend un objet quelconque pour marquer son numéro. Celui qui vient le premier, sur N° 3 met sa marque sur N° 1 et commence le jeu N° 4 avance toute suite sur N° 15. N° 6 paye 2 mq. N° 10 reçoit 5 mq. et avance sur N° 13. N° 12 recule sur N° 7. N° 18 paye 4 mq. N° 9 reçoit 6 mq. et avance sur N° 21. N° 19 aide si longtemps décharger la voiture jusqu'à ce qu'autre joueurs y joigne et le remplace. Dans la cuisine on s'arrête jusqu'à ce qu'on fait 3 points, alors on a gagné le jeu et reçoit tout ce qu'il y a dans la caisse et s'assied sur la chaise préparée et mange. Les numéros 2. 5. 8. 11. 14. 17. 20. 23. payent tous 1 mq. d'amende. Celui qui jette plus de 25 recule d'autant qu'il a fait trop de points.

Morals and Religion: How to Behave!

In England, games intended for the moral education of young people were widely available. Even those not explicitly designed with a moral theme could be repurposed for such intent. By contrast, France predominantly produced games with religious and spiritual themes.

While educational games were popular in eighteenth-century France, the trend for these games in England only emerged towards the century's end. The game that arguably kickstarted this trend was actually a pirated version of a French game, 'The New Game of Human Life,' which aptly opens this chapter. This game had a strong moral undertone and wielded significant influence. Within a few decades following the turn of the century, all major English game producers had embraced the trend, releasing numerous games intended for 'moral improvement' alongside a variety of other printed games. These were premium products, intricately engraved and hand-colored – often by children coerced into labor. These children would sit in circles, each specializing in applying a specific color with fine brushes, passing the game sheet from one to the next.

Priced at approximately seven shillings, one of these English games, luxuriously housed in a mahogany box complete with a teetotum and 'pillars' (colored wooden pawns marking a player's position on the game sheet), could amount to a significant portion of a skilled craftsman's weekly earnings. Consequently, these were high-end games with limited sales. Nowadays, they rank among the rarest games available. Highly coveted by collectors, many exist in such limited quantities that finding complete sets, inclusive of their rule-books and gaming equipment, is nearly impossible, even within museum collections.

English games often touted moral superiority for including a teetotum instead of dice. For instance, a footnote in 'The New Game of Human Life' reads: 'It is necessary to inform the Purchaser the Totum must be marked with the Figures 1 2 3 4 5 6 & to avoid introducing a Dice Box into private Families, each player must spin twice, which will answer the same purpose.' A more pragmatic reason for supplying an unmarked teetotum was sidestepping the exorbitant tax on dice in Georgian England: double dice would incur a 20-shilling tax, more than twice the game's price.

A recurring feature in these moral games was the emphasis on charitable donations and altruistic actions towards the less fortunate, underscoring the games' target audience: the wealthy upper class. Encouraging philanthropy, even from an early age, was deemed essential. Notably, games from English Quaker family publishers often injected moral messages into seemingly mundane-themed games. Hence, even avian behavior might impart a moral lesson, or an exploration of London's landmarks could evoke contemplations on the detrimental impacts of colonialism, the East India Company, and the inherent value of money. Some of these moralistic English games were overwhelmingly somber, unlikely to brighten even a dreary weekend. However, others struck

a balance, designed to entertain children while simultaneously imparting ethical lessons.

In the predominantly Roman Catholic France, games with a spiritual lens were favored. Some were explicitly crafted to educate children entering religious orders, while others, like the 'Moral and Instructive' game discussed here, targeted a broader audience. These often delved into the nuances of sin, advocating repentance and the adoption of specific virtues as antidotes. Some games adopted a surprisingly straightforward approach to religious symbolism. For instance, one game (not discussed here) transforms the Stations of the Cross into the traditional Goose spaces, doubling the roll. This chapter highlights the contrasting perspectives on religion between England and France.

The chapter wraps up with the delightful 'Willy's Walk to see Grandmamma.' In this game, players won't encounter profound moral or spiritual teachings – only lessons in good behavior and kindness.

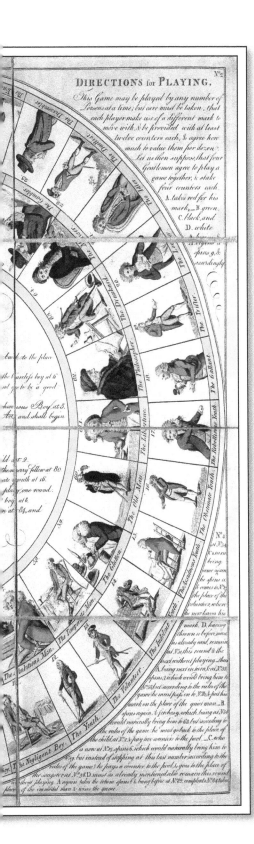

The New Game of Human Life.
London: Newbery and Wallis
1790

'The New Game of Human Life' is an adaptation of the Game of the Goose, expanded to 84 spaces to depict the seven ages of man, each spanning 12 years. The 'age' spaces, numbered 12, 24, and so on, function as Goose spaces, doubling the roll. Its distinction as a 'moral' game is grounded in its various hazard spaces. For instance, the *Prodigal* at space 30 is obliged to pay four stakes and revert to space 6, labeled the *Careless Boy*. True to their names, the Prodigal is illustrated squandering his money, while the Careless Boy is preoccupied with building a house of cards – a symbolic representation of futile endeavors. The publishers behind this game were Elizabeth Newbery and John Wallis. Newbery, a prominent publisher of children's materials, likely advocated for the prominent claim to the 'Utility and Moral Tendency of this Game' showcased at the upper left of the board. The game itself mirrors a version released by Crépy in Paris a decade and a half prior, though alterations were implemented for the English audience. The pinnacle space showcases Sir Isaac Newton in lieu of the more contentious figure, Voltaire, featured in the French edition. A pronounced caricature of George, the Prince Regent, is displayed at space 57, denoted as the *Ambitious Man*. Meanwhile, Captain Cook, the renowned explorer, is depicted alongside his globe at space 47, embodying the Geographer.

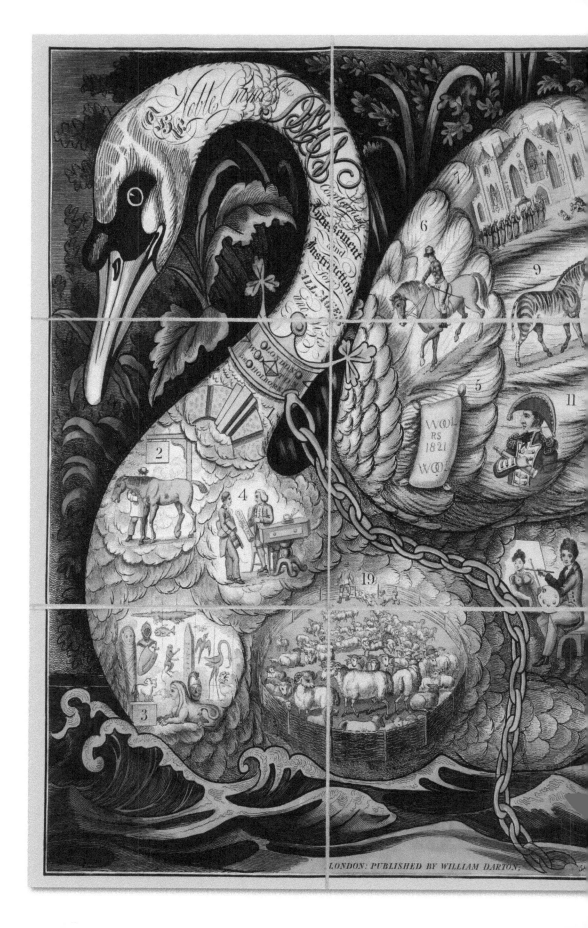

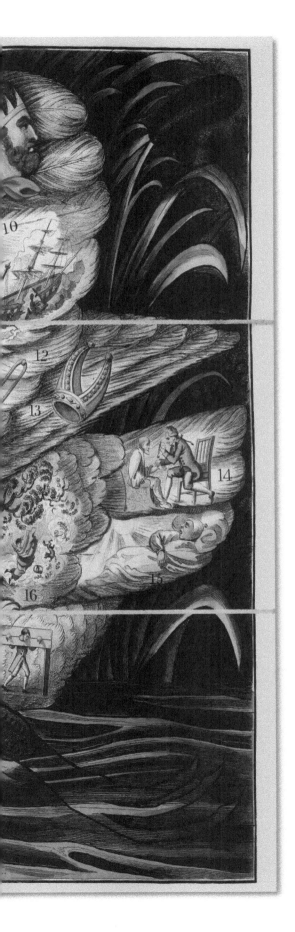

The next example is a fine Darton engraving, beautifully hand-colored: *The Noble Game of the Swan – Providing Amusement and Instruction for All Ages and Sizes*. However, the subjects depicted offer quite a peculiar assortment. The track begins with images of a keystone, a post horse, a museum, a merchant, a wool pack, a jockey, and an abbey – there's no apparent link between them. The booklet that comes with the game offers descriptions of each subject, often with a patriotic slant. For instance, regarding space 5, it notes, 'Wool is the primary sector of our trade with other nations, and English woolen fabrics are unrivaled.' By space 15, moral lessons emerge, exemplified by the sluggard: 'What can one say about this individual, whose very name draws disdain?' Yet, perhaps the most evident moral lesson is the booklet's warning against cheating, be it by manipulating the teetotum or the game piece!

The Novel and Elegant Game of the Basket of Fruit.
London: Darton
1845

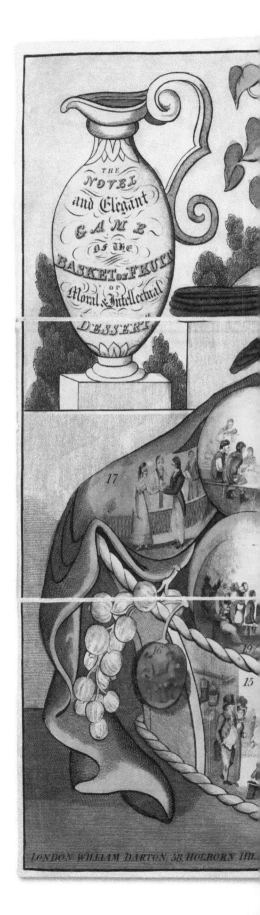

Darton's *Game of the Basket of Fruit*, while exquisitely designed, presents an eclectic array of subjects. The scenes include: 1. Penitentiary, 2. Trial by Jury, 3. Home Visits to the Indigent, 4. Students at the Royal Academy, 5. Exhibition at the Royal Academy, 6. A Clinic, 7. A Retirement Home, 8. A Chemistry Lecture, 9. A Blue-coat Boy, 10. A Public School, 11. Confirmation, 12. A Bazaar, 13. Greenwich Retirees, 14. Women's Charitable Society, 15. School for the Blind, 16. Chelsea Veterans, 17. Marriage, 18. Harvest Celebration, 19. A Bible Society, 20. Glory spurring on an Oxonian and a Cantab student in Academics and the Arts.

The Dartons were Quakers, and the descriptions of the various scenes in the accompanying booklet reflect their beliefs and philosophies. For instance, the commentary on the Women's Charitable Society procession reveals the Quakers' aversion to public ostentation: '… we're inclined to believe that these kind-hearted women might seem more fitting seated in dialogue for the society's betterment rather than parading the streets with colorful banners.' This likely wasn't the most lively game on the shelf!

The Swan of Elegance. London: Harris
1814

Compared to the earlier Darton games, *The Swan of Elegance* published by John Harris is a decidedly more cheerful game. Scenes of children either behaving well or misbehaving decorate a crimson ribbon adorning a magnificent swan. Each scene is paired with a moralizing verse in the accompanying booklet. Space 23 features *Gluttonous Helen* — 'Here's Helen, nearly choking from eating mince pies, / Isn't it a shame she's so greedy? / She must go back to Charles to learn a lesson, / And deposit three counters in the bank.' Sure enough, at space 9, we witness 'Frugal Charles' slicing a very thin piece from a large frosted cake. Space 10 introduces 'Deceitful Harriet,' who has broken a dish and is attempting to blame the cat. Her deceit gets her nowhere: she's required to pay four counters to the bank and skip three turns.

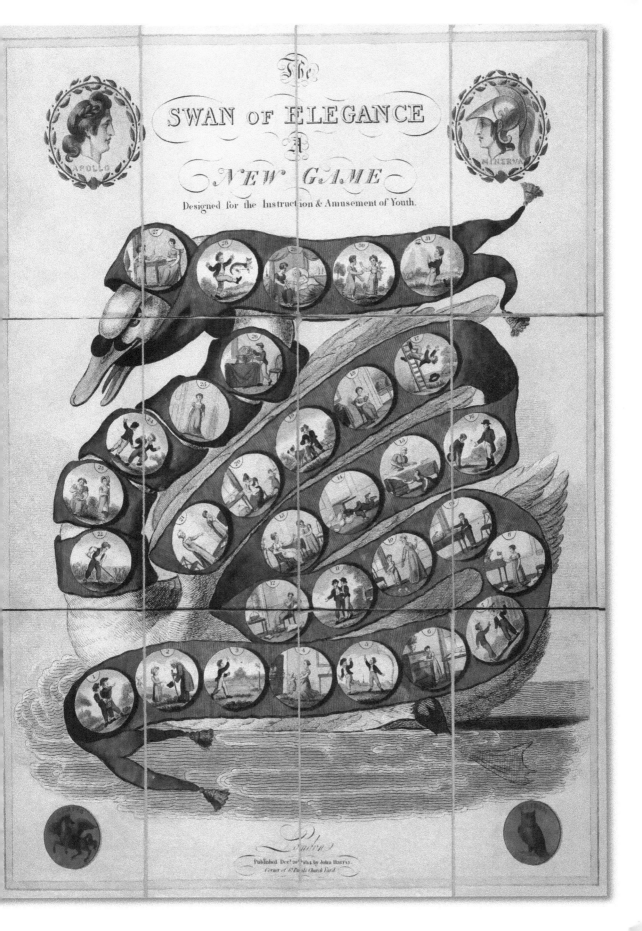

British and Foreign Birds. London: Darton

1820

'A NEW GAME MORAL, INSTRUCTIVE, AND AMUSING DESIGNED to ENTICE the MINDS of YOUTH to an ACQUAINTANCE with the WONDERS OF NATURE' – proclaims, in grand style, the subtitle of the Darton game of *British and Foreign Birds*. The engraved playing track consists of 25 spaces, each showcasing a bird. These are connected by the body of an imposing snake, complete with a forked tail, forked tongue, and an intimidating set of curved teeth. It's uncertain what impact this daunting decoration had on the 'minds of youth' – it certainly doesn't pertain to the game itself. The rule booklet dedicates a separate page to each bird, expecting the player to reference it for a description, which must have made the game's pace quite leisurely. For several of the spaces, instructions are provided that seem to embody the character of the bird, aiming to highlight a moral lesson. Space 2: The *Peacock* — pause one turn to admire the exquisite plumage of this bird and mock its vanity. Space 7: *The Ostrich* — the spinner can't match the ostrich's speed; therefore, spin again. Space 8: *The Parrot* — the player should move back three spaces for talking excessively. The Eagle, the 'majestic and renowned bird,' graces the winning space.

A Survey of London by a Party of Tarry-at-Home Travelers. London: Darton

1820

How on Earth can a game about the public buildings of London be used to instill moral values? This challenge was not insurmountable for the Dartons with their game, *A Survey of London by a Party of Stay-at-Home Travelers*. Their Quaker values are on full display in the booklet, which offers extensive descriptions of the seventeen buildings portrayed. A visit to the Mint (space 12) provokes the remark: 'The sight of such riches may invoke wonder; but one should remember that wealth comes with its burdens.' It continues to 'advise my young friends' that their New Year's shilling (a customary gift for kids in affluent families), valued at twelve cents, might be better spent providing a 'modest meal' for an equal number of needy and hungry individuals. However, the booklet's most potent moral commentary is reserved for the East India Company. Their museum, found at space 7, showcases numerous items taken from their original proprietors: 'We could have spared the thousands of Eastern natives who have suffered due to our misguided ambition and unwarranted claims on their property and land holdings.' Such candid anti-colonial sentiments were rare in Georgian London.

Moral and Instructive Game.
Nancy: Jarville
about 1890

This 'moral and instructive' French game is, in fact, a religious game. It originates from around 1860, though the version displayed is a reprint produced towards the end of the century. Its 63-space track culminates in Paradise, showcasing God the Father, flanked by images of the Blessed Virgin Mary and Jesus. The hazard spaces correspond to various sins. The cardinal sins present the player with a choice between paying a stake to the pool or returning to the corresponding virtue opposed to the sin – a rare instance where a choice of movement is allowed in a Goose-type game. Landing on other virtues doubles the throw, similar to a goose space. Other sins impose penalties familiar in the original game. As always with such games, it's intriguing to see the treatment of the *death* space. Here, it's Pride (experiencing a downfall at space 58), with the typical 'start over' rule. Oddly, the game's designer forgot to provide a rule for the sin of Envy, vividly depicted at space 44 where one man violently beats another with a club. Aside from this oversight, the designer chose to populate the non-active spaces with illustrations of rural trades and occupations, which contrast innocuously with the intense spiritual scenes portrayed elsewhere.

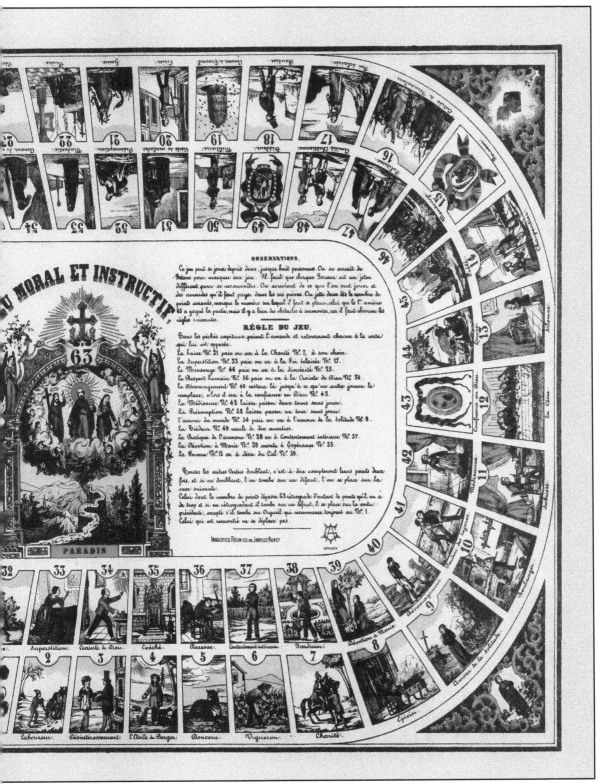

U MORAL ET INSTRUCTIF.

63

PARADIS.

OBSERVATIONS.

Ce jeu peut se jouer depuis deux, jusque huit personnes. On se munit de Jetons pour marquer son jeu. Il faut que chaque Joueur ait un jeton différent pour se reconnaître. On convient de ce que l'on veut jouer et des amendes qu'il faut payer dans les cas prévus. On jette deux dés le nombre de points amenés, marque le numéro sur lequel il faut se placer, celui qui le 1er amène 63 a gagné la partie, mais il y a bien des obstacles à surmonter, car il faut observer les règles suivantes.

RÈGLE DU JEU.

Tous les péchés capitaux paient l'amende et retournent chacun à la vertu qui lui est opposé.

La haine N°. 21 paie ou va à la Charité N°. 7, à son choix.
La Superstition N°. 33 paie ou va à la Foi éclairée N°. 17.
Le Mensonge N°. 46 paie ou va à la Sincérité N°. 25.
Le Respect humain N°. 56 paie ou va à la Crainte de Dieu N°. 34.
Le Découragement N°. 40 restera là jusqu'à ce qu'un autre joueur le remplace, alors il ira à la confiance en Dieu N°. 43.
La Médisance N°. 42 laisse passer deux tours sans jouer.
La Présomption N°. 52 laisse passer un tour sans jouer.
L'amour du monde N°. 54 paie ou va à l'amour de la solitude N°. 9.
La Tiédeur N°. 49 recule de dix numéros.
La Pratique de l'aumône N°. 28 va à Contentement intérieur N°. 37.
La Dévotion à Marie N°. 39 monte à Espérance N°. 55.
La Ferveur N°. 15 va à Désir du Ciel N°. 59.

Toutes les autres Vertus doublent, c'est-à-dire compteront leurs points deux fois, et si en doublant, l'on tombe sur un défaut, l'on se place sur la case suivante.
Celui dont le nombre de points dépasse 63 rétrograde d'autant de points qu'il en a de trop et en rétrogradant il tombe sur un défaut, il se place sur la vertu précédente, excepté s'il tombe sur Orgueil qui recommence toujours au N°. 1.
Celui qui est rencontré ne se déplace pas.

IMAGERIES REUNIES DE JARVILLE-NANCY

DÉPOSÉE.

Willy's Walk to see Grandmamma.
London: Myers
1869

'**W**illy's Walk to see Grandmamma' is a light-hearted game designed to entertain children. It features a 79-space track, with Grandmamma's house at the center. This game hails from 1869, five decades after the earnest and 'educational' games like those by the Dartons. Here, the mishaps during the journey aren't menacing, and the moral lessons are suggested, not spelled out overtly. Some of the hazards echo those of the Goose game. At space 20, Willy falls down and must wait for someone to help him up or forfeit two turns. Other spaces depict realistic distractions a young boy might encounter during a trip – purchasing apples, gathering flowers, forgetting his package requiring a return trip, engaging in a game of marbles, and so forth. Conversely, hitching a ride in the baker's cart or hopping on the omnibus propels him forward. Intriguingly, when Willy performs a virtuous act, like offering a poor child an apple or urging some boys not to taunt a dog, he must skip a turn or two. In earlier games, there would've been a clear incentive to underscore a moral lesson by rewarding his commendable actions.

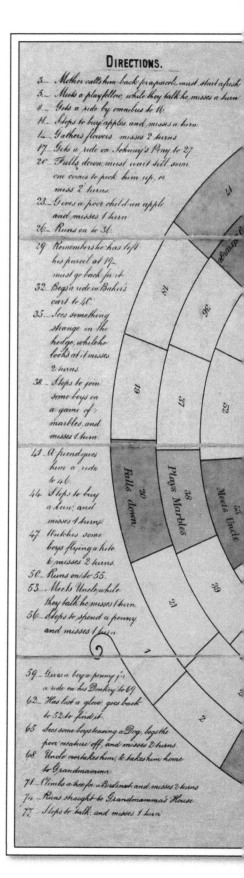

DIRECTIONS.

3.— Mother calls him back for a parcel, must start afresh
5.— Meets a playfellow, while they talk he misses a turn
8.— Gets a ride by omnibus to 16.
11.— Stops to buy apples, and misses a turn.
14.— Gathers flowers misses 2 turns
17.— Gets a ride on Johnny's Pony to 27
20.— Falls down must wait till some one comes to pick him up, or miss 2 turns.
23.— Gives a poor child an apple and misses 1 turn
26.— Runs on to 31.
29.— Remembers he has left his parcel at 19. must go back for it
33.— Begs a ride in Baker's cart to 40.
35.— Sees something strange in the hedge, while he looks at it misses 2 turns.
38.— Stops to join some boys in a game of marbles, and misses 1 turn.
41.— A friend gives him a ride to 46.
44.— Stops to buy a bun, and misses 1 turn.
47.— Watches some boys flying a kite & misses 2 turns.
50.— Runs on to 55.
53.— Meets Uncle, while they talk he misses 1 turn.
56.— Stops to spend a penny and misses 1 turn.
59.— Gives a boy a penny for a ride on his Donkey to 69.
62.— Has lost a glove, goes back to 52 to find it.
65.— Sees some boys teasing a Dog, begs the poor creature off, and misses 2 turns.
68.— Uncle overtakes him, & takes him home to Grandmamma
71.— Climbs a tree for a Bird's nest and misses 2 turns.
74.— Runs straight to Grandmamma's House
77.— Stops to talk and misses 1 turn.

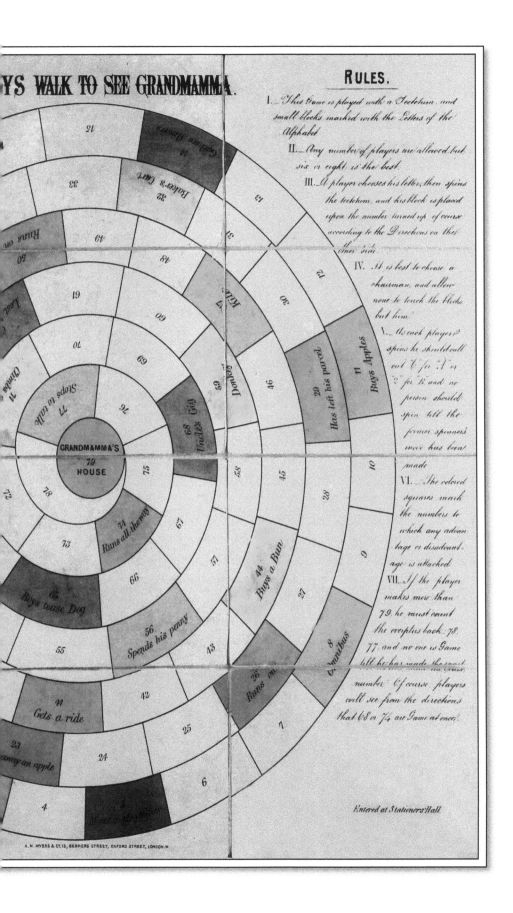

RULES.

I.—This Game is played with a Teetotum and small blocks marked with the Letters of the Alphabet.

II.—Any number of players are allowed, but six or eight is the best.

III.—A player chooses his letter, then spins the teetotum, and his block is placed upon the number turned up, of course according to the Directions on the other side.

IV.—It is best to choose a chairman, and allow none to touch the blocks but him.

V.—As each player spins he should call out C for A or B for B, and no person should spin till the former spinner's move has been made.

VI.—The colored squares mark the numbers to which any advantage or disadvantage is attached.

VII.—If the player makes more than 79, he must count the overplus back; 78, 77, and no one is Game till he has made the exact number. Of course players will see from the directions that 68 or 74 are Game at once.

Entered at Stationers' Hall

A. N. MYERS & Cᵒ. 15, BERNERS STREET, OXFORD STREET, LONDON. W.

Journeys: Where Shall We Go?

Journey games gained immense popularity in Germany, initially featuring the stagecoach but transitioning to trains and steamships as the century progressed. The 18th-century English games, which were based on a map of the Grand Tour of Europe, evolved in the 19th century into voyages around the world.

While the Game of the Goose can be interpreted as symbolizing life's journey, the journeys in this chapter focus on imaginative travel from one destination to another. The earliest of these is the Post and Journey Game, which originated in Germany in the late 18th century. In these games, a horse-drawn carriage's journey culminates in the central city, after navigating the many obstacles characteristic of that challenging travel era. These games maintain their distinct rules, diverging from direct adaptations

of the Game of the Goose, yet share many generic similarities. Players progress through advantageous spaces and encounter a plethora of obstacles that hinder movement. The rules cleverly emulate real-life travel's delays and frustrations. And, mirroring the Game of the Goose, these are dice games that don't offer a choice of move.

The 19th century's fascination with emerging transportation forms birthed games dedicated to innovations like the steam ferry or the railway. Many games were remarkably specific, detailing journeys between named places, aiming to captivate a local audience. Some introduced novel rules to simulate the experience of new transportation forms. Others delved into the technicalities, showcasing diverse railway rolling stock or illustrating track-side equipment and other railway structures. Historians often find these games invaluable, given their meticulous depictions.

Another journey game category highlights prominent destinations, whether they're a city's public landmarks or significant stops on a lengthier expedition. These games evolved from the geographical ones discussed in Chapter 3. A notable theme is a global voyage. While such games have been around since the early 19th century, Jules Verne's 1873 novel, 'Around the World in Eighty Days,' invigorated this genre. The book not only inspired games illustrating the fictional journey of Phileas Fogg but also games portraying real-world voyages. These mirrored the growing allure of tourism. Yet, entirely imaginative journeys remained beloved – like board games exploring the stars.

This chapter's journey games showcase an array of production techniques. 'The Traveler in Europe' game, printed via detailed copper plate engraving, epitomizes the Parisian printing houses that catered to the aristocracy's heirs in earlier centuries. This stands in stark contrast to the low-cost woodcut of the 'Dutch Steamboat' game, printed on flimsy paper. Though both emerged in the 19th century's early years, they targeted distinct demographics. Mid-century saw the advent of lithography (printing from flat stones using greasy ink), gradually replacing engraving. 'The Orient' game exemplifies the impeccable – albeit costly – outcomes possible when merging this technique with intricate hand coloring. As the century waned, chromolithography emerged, facilitating vibrant game sheets like 'Round the World in Eighty Days' and more affordable ones like the 'Italian World Tour.'

New Post and Journey Game. Nuremberg: Campe

about 1820

We start with a *New Post and Journey* game from around 1820, made in Nuremberg, Germany – a city that would become pivotal in the production of toys and games for global markets. The initial space displays the stagecoach embarking on its journey toward the central destination: a walled city by the river, which might very well represent Nuremberg on the River Pegnitz.

Unlike the Game of the Goose, there aren't any throw-doubling spaces. Instead, the journey is segmented into stages, with a station every ten spaces. When landing on such a station, the player moves to the next. There's a counterpart to the death space found in the Goose game: at space 37, the coach encounters an accident, and the player has to start over. This game features a unique water hazard at space 53, serving as a blockade. If the player lands here without first accessing the 'boat' at space 51, they lose the game. Any points thrown beyond 53 count backward, and the player can't move on without first stopping at the boat space. This clever twist on the Goose game's finishing rule injects a dose of realism into the perceived journey.

Zum Anfang zahlt jeder 24 Marggen Postgeld, und steigt bei N°1 in den Reisewagen. Kommt man auf eine Station, so setzt man sein Zeichen auf die nächste. Wenn man in ein Wirthshaus kommt, so muß man 4 Marg Zeche bezahlen. Bey N°3, dem Schlagbaum, kostet es 2 Marg Weggeld. Der Meilenzeiger N°7. gewinnt 3 Marg. Die Allee N°9. gewinnt 4. Der Berg N°13. verl. 2 Marg. Die Wiese N°16. gewinnt 5 Marg. Das Dorf N°18. gewinnt 4 Marg. Der Wald N°21. verliert 3 Marg. Der Räuber N°25. plündert ein 12 Marg. Dem Bettler N°27. giebt man 1 Marg. Das Posthorn N°31. gewinnt 6 Marg. In der Mühle N°33. zahlt man fürs Nachtquartier 3 Marg. Zerbricht der Wagen N°37. so muß man wieder von vorn anfangen. Bey der Brücke N°42. giebt man 2 Marg Zoll. Das Kornfeld N°44. gew. 5 Marg. Die Ritterburg N°47. verliert 3 Marg. Wer in die Ueberschwemmung geräth, ohne vorher in den Kahn N°51. sich gesetzt zu haben, ersäuft, und hat das Spiel verloren, fällt aber der Wurf darüber, so zählt man das Uebrige von N°53. zurück, bis man endlich in den Kahn kommt, und nur dann kann man wieder reisen. In dem Kloster N°57. opfert man 2 Marggen. Der Postillon N°59. erhält 8 Marggen Trinkgeld. Derjenige so am ersten in der Hauptstadt N°61. anlangt, ist Gewinner des ganzen Spiels.

94

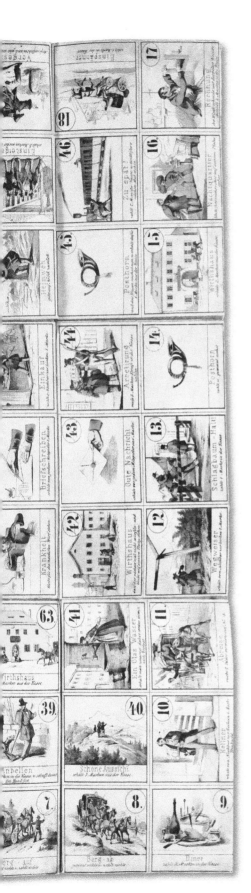

Railway and Steamship Game.
Stuttgart: Hoffmann
about 1850

The *Railway and Steamship* game offers a mid-century twist on the classic Post and Journey game. This 85-space rectangular track, with rules detailed in every space, ends in a joyful touchdown at the train station. Initially, the journey isn't modernized, and the modes of transportation resemble those of its predecessor. Contemporary readers will find intrigue in the snapshots of daily life – for instance, space 17 illustrates how an inn keeps tabs using a chalkboard. A less-than-pleasant turn of events occurs at space 27 due to a highway robbery, forcing the player to give up 6 stakes and backtrack to the prior town. The traveler misses his train at space 46 but luckily boards it at the very next space. By space 54, as he's walking, he realizes there's a hole in his shoes and needs a fix. Fast forward to space 58, he reaches a port, and in the succeeding space, braves a treacherous gangway to get on the steam-powered ferry. The scene in the cabin at space 61 isn't exactly heartening – with some passengers seemingly battling seasickness – but everyone disembarks unharmed. Reaching space 64, our traveler feels the onset of illness and must resort to a tonic. At space 68, he hops onto a mail coach, and after a brief encounter with customs at the border, he reaches his endpoint. Essentially, this game paints a tale of overcoming travel-related challenges.

Steamboat Game. Arnhem: De Jong

about 1835

The *Steamboat Game* is a two-dice race game centered on the steam ferry that traveled between Amsterdam and Zaandam, situated just across the river – nowadays, it's a five-minute train ride. The depicted boat is the Mercurius, constructed in 1824, and it started its route between Amsterdam and Zaandam in 1826. It's likely the game was introduced in the subsequent decade. The end goal of the unconventional 60-space track is the Czaar Peterhuisje, the historic residence of Peter the Great in Zaandam. The onboard accommodations for the first, second, and third class are highlighted at spaces 7, 9, and 11. An accompanying rule sheet details the costs for these spaces: 5, 3, and 2 cents, respectively. Additional charges are incurred for a new pipe of tobacco, a glass of *Jenever* (Dutch gin), and a cup of coffee. Along the way, you might need to pay at the Willemsluis, the William I lock linking to the North Holland Canal. If you end up in Zaandam, you're out. Proceeding further might require hiring a horse carriage and a porter for your luggage, and if you choose to lodge at the inn, there are additional fees. Despite this print being a modest woodcut, its straightforward charm is undeniable.

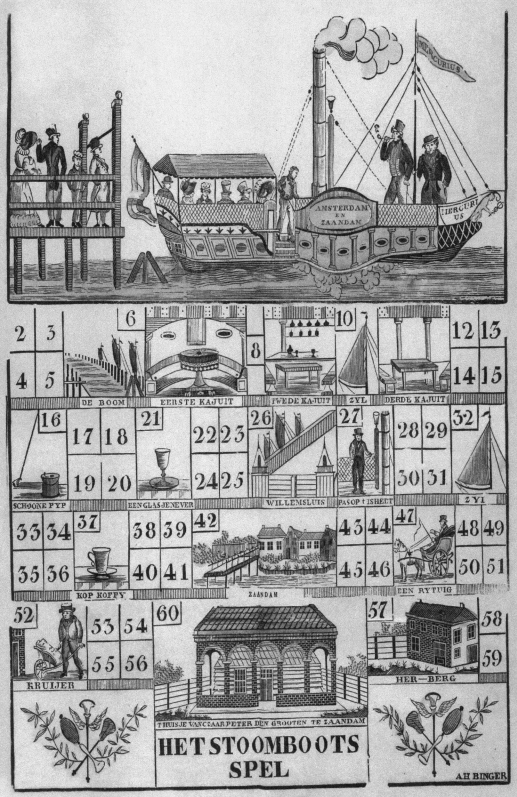

HET STOOMBOOTS SPEL

NEDERLANDSCHE RIJNSPOORWEG-GEZELSCHAPSSPEL.

Uitgave van D. Allart/De Bezige Bij, te Amsterdam.

Rhine Railway Game.
Amsterdam: Allart
about 1870

The *Rhine Railway Game* is inspired by an actual transportation system and celebrates the Nederlandsche Rijnspoorweg-Maatschappij (NRS). This company constructed a route from Amsterdam to Utrecht, which opened in 1843, extended it to Arnhem, and finally reached Germany by 1856. The game itself hit the market in 1874. Its track spans 63 spaces, identical in length to the Game of the Goose, though the rules differ in detail. The portrayal of the train, especially towards the end of the track, is striking. Following the locomotive and tender are the conductor's car and the mail car, succeeded by the first-, second-, and several third-class coaches, and concluding with the freight, livestock, and flatbed cars. The illustrations of the numerous stations en route stand out due to their unique character and serve as a valuable historical record. Produced using chromolithography, this game's vibrant and appealing colors were realized at a fraction of the cost compared to manual coloring.

Game of the Traveler in Europe.
Paris: Basset
1830

❧

In the *Game of the Traveler in Europe*, players are taken to Europe's most iconic landmarks. This 63-space game is heavily influenced by the 'Game of the Goose.' Along the path, players encounter intricate depictions of Europe's renowned structures. The beneficial Goose-like spaces, where players can double their move, feature cathedrals and other significant churches. The *bridge* at the sixth space prominently displays London's Westminster Bridge. Other standard obstacles have been thoughtfully adapted to the theme: the *death* space depicts the tomb of the Queen of Denmark; the *well* space showcases Seville, Spain's aqueduct; and the *prison* space presents the imposing fortress in Lille, crafted by Vauban. The original version of this game emerged during Napoleon I's imperial era. However, following his abdication and the subsequent return of the Bourbons, the term 'imperial' in the game's text had to be switched to 'royal' to stay politically correct. Instead of incurring the cost of creating a new engraving, modifications were made directly to the existing printing plate. A keen eye can spot the minor voids where these changes took place.

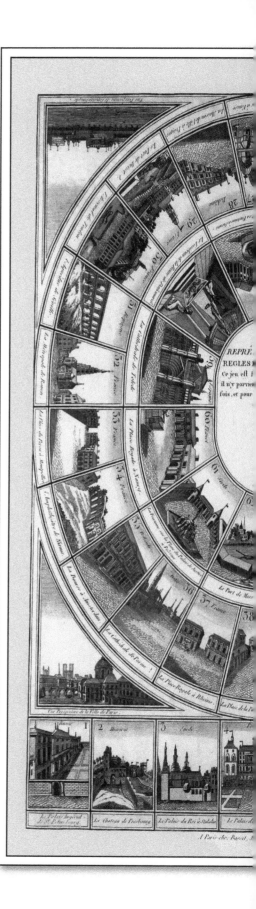

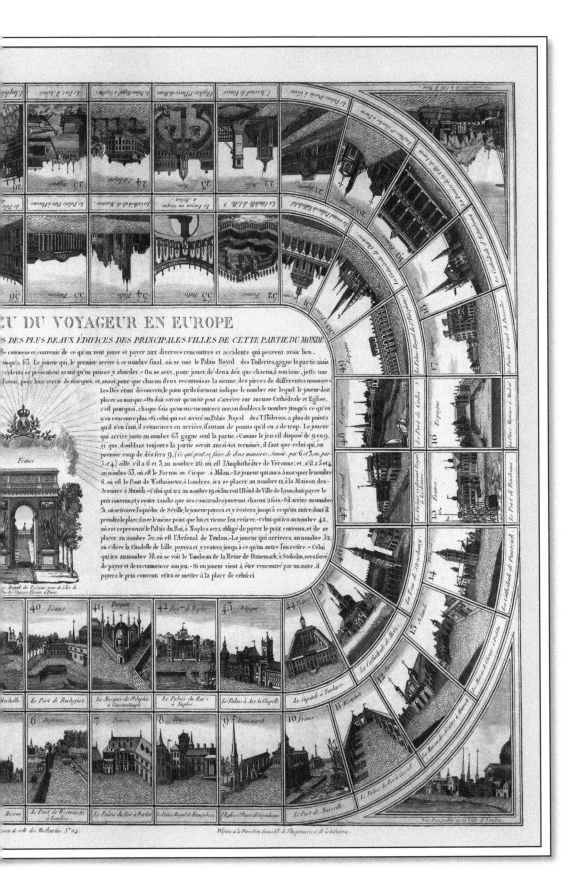

L'Orient, or the Indian Travelers.
London: Ogilvy
1846

L' *Orient, or the Indian Travelers,* stands out as one of the most impressive games crafted in London during the mid-19th century. The artwork is top-notch, likely credited to a renowned artist, J W Barfoot, R.A., and the hand coloring is meticulous – this game was definitely high-end. It actually offers two games in one. The illustrations encircling the central map on its left, right, and bottom depict historical events in India, but predominantly through an English lens. Players select one of the English monarchs displayed above the map. Taking turns, they draw cards from a bag, each card depicting a specific event. The player then identifies the monarch during whose rule the event took place. If correct, they can match the card to the respective event image. Each reign has six events, and the game continues until all events under one monarch are matched. The player representing that monarch emerges as the winner.

The second game is more of a race, following one of three mapped routes: the overland path through Marseilles (highlighted in red); the overland route via Trieste (in yellow); or the sea route, navigating around the Cape of Good Hope. Gameplay is steered by a teetotum, a spinning top with colored sides, moving the player along the route matching the color that's face up. Intriguingly, the rules suggest that those living in India can opt for Calcutta as their starting point, instead of London. This truly embodies a game from the pinnacle of the British Colonial era.

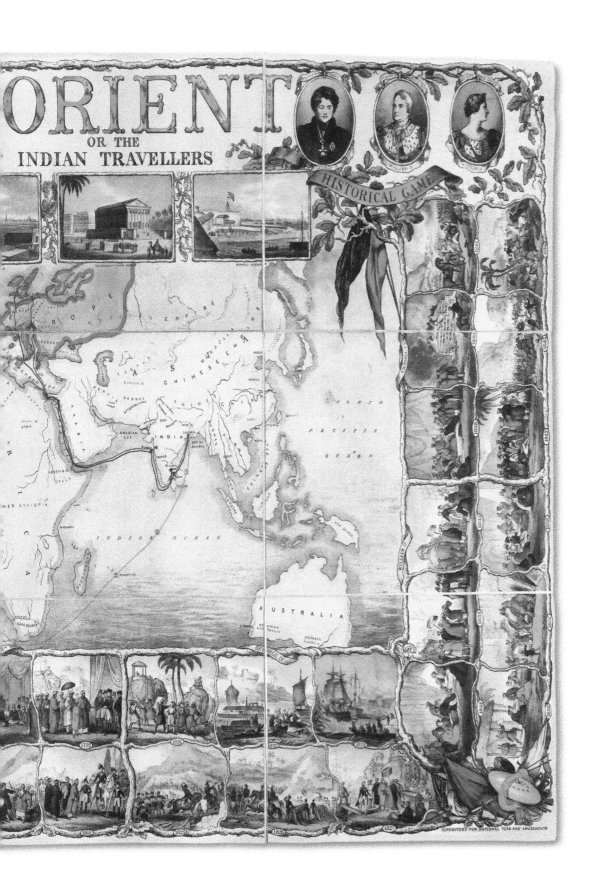

Round the World in

Eighty Days.

Paris: JJF

about 1906

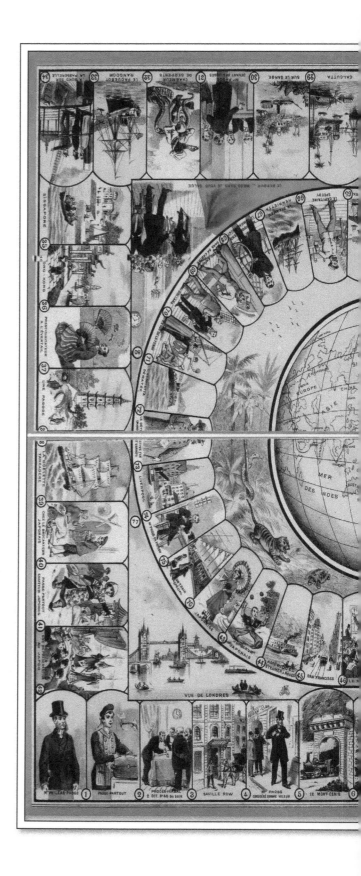

J ules Verne's adventure novel, *Around the World in Eighty Days*, was published in France in 1873. The tale chronicles the journey of Phileas Fogg, a London gentleman, who aims to circumnavigate the globe with his French valet, Passe-partout, on a £20,000 wager. The story gained immense popularity, leading to the release of several board games inspired by the narrative. The game featured here, an exquisite chromolithograph, was introduced somewhat later, in 1906. An 80-space track, representing each day of the journey, encircles a central world map depicting the duo's route. The final four spaces are situated in the corners, bridging the outer and inner sections of the track. Among the numerous adventures illustrated, one of the most thrilling happens at space 59. Here, the traveler gets captured by Native Americans and must await rescue by another player, mirroring the 'prison' rule of the Goose game.

III

a *Suez*, cioè al N. 15, deve pagare il diritto di passaggio alla Compagnia del Canale e va direttamente in *Aden*, cioè al N. 20. — Chi va al N. 21, entra in *Quarantena*, e sta un giro senza giocare. — Chi va al N. 31, trova i *Questurini* del Regno di Siam che si insospettiscono di lui, e lo mettano in prigione. Deve quindi stare cola finchè sia cavato da un altro, con cui cambia il posto. Se nessuno arriva, dopo un giro, paga ancora la posta e tira innanzi. — Chi va al N. 42 trova i *Pirati Chinesi*, e per non esser preso, scappa indietro sino a *Sydney* in Australia, cioè al N. 37, pagando il convenuto. — Chi va al N. 52 trova una *Burrasca terribile* che lo rimanda a *Bombay* nelle Indie Inglesi, cioè al N. 22. — Chi va al N. 71 deve pagare il dazio a *Liverpool*, per la

Tour of the World.
Milan: Bertarelli

about 1890

With its 80-space track, Bertarelli's *Tour of the World* game was evidently influenced by Verne's novel. However, this game charts a real journey rather than a fictional one. The text in the upper left of the game sheet clarifies that the gameplay is inspired by a route recommended by the Society for Study Tours around the World [SVEAM], a travel agency headquartered in Paris and established in 1878. The Goose spaces feature dangerous animals, and players must immediately retreat from these, adhering to the standard rule of doubling their throw. In a touch of realism, the Suez Canal (space 15) directly transports travelers to Aden. This game, like the Jules Verne game mentioned earlier, presents challenges with Native Americans. However, in this version (space 56), the unfortunate traveler faces a grim fate, getting devoured and subsequently eliminated from the game.

IV

sua entrata in Inghilterra. — Chi al N. 56 cade in potere degli Indiani *Pelli-Rosse* che lo mangiano vivo. È finita per lui, e non gioca più. — Chi passa il N. 80 torna indietro contando i punti fatti in più; se incontra una bestia feroce, indietreggia ancora, ricontando i punti. — Chi va ad un numero in cui v'è già un altro, cambia con questi il posto. — Qualora avvenisse, cosa però non molto probabile, che tutti i giocatori cadessero in mano degli Indiani *Pelli Rosse*, al N. 58, e fossero mangiati vivi, si rimette un'altra posta e si riconlacia il gioco.

Aphelion. London: Ayres
about 1890

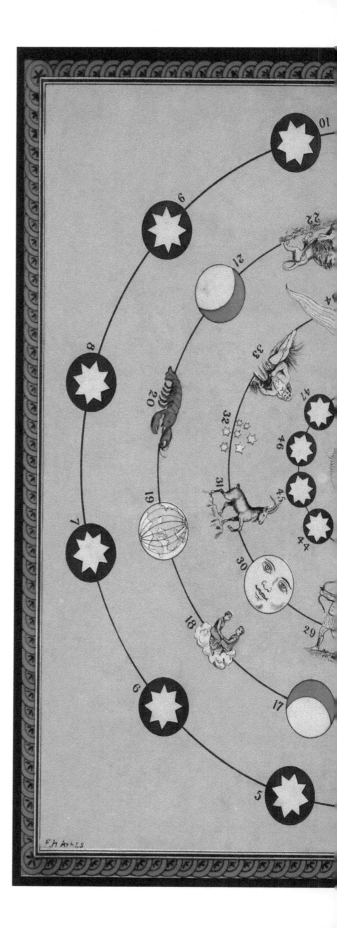

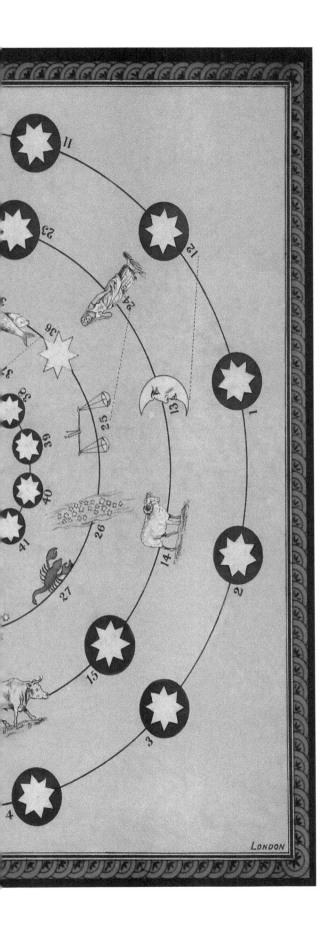

The game of '*Aphelion* [to the Sun]'
is a single-die game that imagines a
journey from the stars to the Sun. Its
track consists of 50 numbered spaces
set within four concentric circles: the
outermost representing fixed stars, the
next two showcasing zodiacal signs, and
the innermost circle representing the
planets. An unusual feature, as noted in
the game's rule leaflet, is that 'the Earth
and Moon have been positioned within
the zodiac circles to enhance enjoyment
and challenge.' The leaflet further
asserts that the game 'will imprint a
lasting impression of the Solar and
Planetary system' on players. One can
only hope that such a peculiar depiction
of astronomy doesn't linger for too long!
Despite these lofty claims, the gameplay
is relatively mundane, primarily
involving straightforward rules about
adding to or taking from a pool of tokens.
However, if a woman lands on space 24
(The Virgin), she is entitled to receive a
token from each man present, in addition
to five from the pool.

Games of War, Siege and Joust: Contests of the Imagination

Games designed to spark interest in the army or navy often included skill-based challenges, like besieging a fortress. In the stunning 'German Game of the Knights,' players faced numerous fairy-tale dangers before proving themselves worthy of the climactic joust.

Educational games centered on the Arts of War first emerged in France towards the end of the 17th century. At that time, every boy from an aristocratic background was expected to learn this subject. The art of fortification was pivotal during this era. In France, boys were taught castle design based on the principles set by the renowned French engineer, Marquis de Vauban (1633-1707). Games centered on the Navy were also popular. While playing, boys not only learned about the perils of the sea but were also introduced to a rich vocabulary related to warships. These board games, showcasing wooden sailing ships, remained popular throughout the 19th century.

For instance, consider 'The New Game of the Imperial Navy.' The original French version of this game was copied in other countries. An English adaptation, 'The Bulwark of Britannia,' was released in 1797. It was essentially the same game but was tailored to the British audience, featuring a central depiction of a 'Sea Fight' which celebrated: 'The glorious victory achieved by Admiral Duncan over the Dutch fleet on October 11, 1797.'

By the close of the 19th century, land warfare had evolved considerably from the era of fortified castles, rendering many older games outdated. New board games emerged, and although many still adhered to the basic design of the Game of the Goose, they mirrored the contemporary shifts in their thematic presentations. For military historians, some of these games are treasured for their meticulous portrayals of soldiering practices of the period, highlighting innovations like the use of bicycles for dispatch delivery.

National pride was at its most evident in these games, regardless of their country of origin. The theme might be the proud military history of that country, or just pride in the regiment of the day. Several games centered on the journey of a young recruit advancing through the ranks to achieve fame and glory as an Admiral or Field-Marshal. That such a positive outcome was a rare event in real-life military service was often glossed over in these games. And, although the games didn't completely ignore the dangers of war, the 'bad spaces' were typically in the minority. These games might not have been specifically designed to recruit young men, but their role in fostering a military culture is undeniable. Games that recounted a specific victorious campaign of the country of origin certainly contributed to this cultural pride.

Yet, combat in board games wasn't always intense. The German 'Ritterspiel' or 'Game of the Knights,' devised at the tail end of the eighteenth century, was conceived as a romantic fairy-tale. Here, aspiring knights faced various challenges and, upon success, awaited another player to challenge in a final, dramatic duel. One might assume this was a game strictly for boys. However, the rules made room for moments of romance, including a scenario where a female player could bestow a chaste kiss.

While the majority of games in this era adopted the familiar roll-and-move model, with movement determined by the roll of dice, there were exceptions. One such game was the Game of Assault – a strategic battle between two players. One player controlled officers defending a castle, while the other controlled rebels attempting to breach it. Games of this kind, with roots in older games like those pitting foxes against geese, highlight how the core mechanics of a game can remain unchanged, even as the surrounding narrative adapts to the times.

The New Game
of the Imperial Navy.
Paris: Basset
about 1810

The *Game of the Imperial Navy* is one of the most captivating reinterpretations of the Game of the Goose. The 63-space spiral symbolizes the journey of a naval ship from departure to its safe arrival at harbor. The beneficial spaces, where the throw is doubled, signify a 'tailwind,' that is, a favorable wind from behind. Another advantageous space is number 6, representing a cape. Navigating around a cape was termed 'doubling' the cape – and fittingly here, the point is doubled to space 12. However, several challenges lie ahead. At space 32, the ship runs aground on a sandbar and needs another ship's assistance. At space 52, the ship gets captured by Corsairs (pirates) and once again requires aid, much like the 'prison' rule of the original game. The equivalent of the *death* space falls at the anticipated space 58, depicting a shipwreck, forcing the player to start over. An educational element is the inclusion of brief definitions of naval terms on the inactive spaces, often accompanied by illustrative images. Oddly enough, the detailed list of ship parts in the central space lacks a corresponding labeled image, perhaps an oversight during the game's update in the Napoleonic era.

PELLERIN & Cᵉ imp.–édit.

JEU HISTORIQUE
DE LA FRANCE MILI...

Premièrement, pour jouer à ce jeu qui est composé de 63 cases, à prendre du n.º 1, où est représentée l'invasion des France, jusqu'au nombre 63, où est l'Arc de triomphe, qui est l'endroit où il ... marque distinctive, afin de ne pas se tromper avec celle de son adversaire, pour marquer sur la case le nombre de points que l'on aura amenés; mais il n'est pas facile d'arriver au nombre 63, car plusieurs ... ce jeu, il faut avoir deux dés que chaque joueur jettera à son tour, et autant de points que les dés amèneront, il les marquera sur le jeu avec sa marque. Il faut bien faire attention que l'on ne peut s'arrêter sur le ... une cabane Vendôme, redoubles le nombre de points que vous avez amenés jusqu'à ce que vous n'en rencontriez plus. Bien marquant les points que vous amenez vers la fin de la partie, vous excédez le nombre 63, r... juste au nombre 63, gagnera la partie.

ARC DE TRIOMPHE

ARC DE TRIOMPHE

63

Historical Game of the French Miltary.
Épinal: Pellerin

about 1860

This historical game chronicles the story of French military prowess throughout the ages. Based on the Game of the Goose, this 63-space game marks every ninth space as favorable, showcasing the Vendôme Column adorned with flags. The column was erected by Napoleon I to commemorate his victory at Austerlitz in 1805 and was crowned by his statue. Even though the column was later demolished by the Paris Commune of the 1870s, who viewed it as a symbol of war and conquest, it was soon rebuilt. Players aim to reach the Arc de Triomphe. The track is decorated with numerous scenes of French victories; for instance, space 4 depicts Clovis, the first King of the Franks, triumphing in battle at Tolbiac around 500 A.D. Hazard spaces include number 15, which illustrates Joan of Arc being captured – adhering to the typical *prison* rule. Others depict French defeats. For instance, space 20 illustrates the French being defeated by the Italian forces at the Battle of Pavia in 1525: players landing there are put out of action and must stay for two turns 'taking care of the wounded' before moving to space 40, Les Invalides in Paris, a hospital for military veterans. Space 55 shows Waterloo (1815) with the rule, 'start over.' The next-to-last space brings the game up to date, illustrating a victory against Austria at the Battle of Solferino in 1859, where French forces led by Napoleon III and Sardinian forces led by Victor-Emmanuel II clashed. This game would not only be fun to play but could also pique players' curiosity about the historical events portrayed.

Game of the Knights. Prague: Fraza
about 1820

This version of the romantic Game of the Knights, printed in Prague for the German market, has instructions written in each of the active spaces, most dictating the player's next move. The story unfolds around a young man's quest for knighthood as he journeys along the outer track. Various challenges await players. To cross the water at space 11, you must roll doubles. You'll come across wizards – some helpful, while others are less so. At the inn (space 19), you pay for lodging but can roll again. Winning your spurs at space 33 also grants another roll. Players should watch out for the 'unhappy' space at number 60, where a dismounted knight is shown, signaling that you must begin the game anew. On a brighter note, if you make it to space 61, you'll be knighted and can enter the final contest. However, before you can start, you must wait for another player to achieve knighthood, who then becomes your adversary. The two knights then duel it out on the central track of 24 small squares. In this section, it's sudden death – if you land on a skull, your opponent wins. Other versions of the game come with intricate rule books. They make it clear that the game was envisioned for both young men and women, where sometimes the young knight might win a kiss from his damsel.

117

The Regiment.
Designed by Ludovic.
Paris: Mauclair-Dacier
about 1895

This detailed chromolithograph illustrates the journey of a young recruit advancing through the ranks of the French army. The meticulous portrayal of uniforms exemplifies the rich detail of this game. The depictions of army life extend beyond just battles and parades. Early in the track, we witness the lottery system determining conscription and the subsequent medical check-up – one potential recruit seems to have bow legs and might not make the cut. The arrival at the regiment and even the mundane tasks like spit-and-polish, referenced as 'l'astiquage' at space 20, are included. A 'bad turnout' leads to a penalty at space 22. As the track progresses, players encounter modern technologies: a dispatch-rider on a bicycle, telegraph operators (utilizing wired communication over radio), and the use of a military balloon for artillery observation.

However, it's the deeply human moments that resonate: a reservist at space 52 bidding farewell to his wife and newborn, the joyous reunions during leaves, the somber reality of falling in battle at space 58, and the shame of demotion captured at space 64. The end goal is Victory, where a thankful community greets the Regiment as heroes. It's a game that's as much a visual feast as it is an activity.

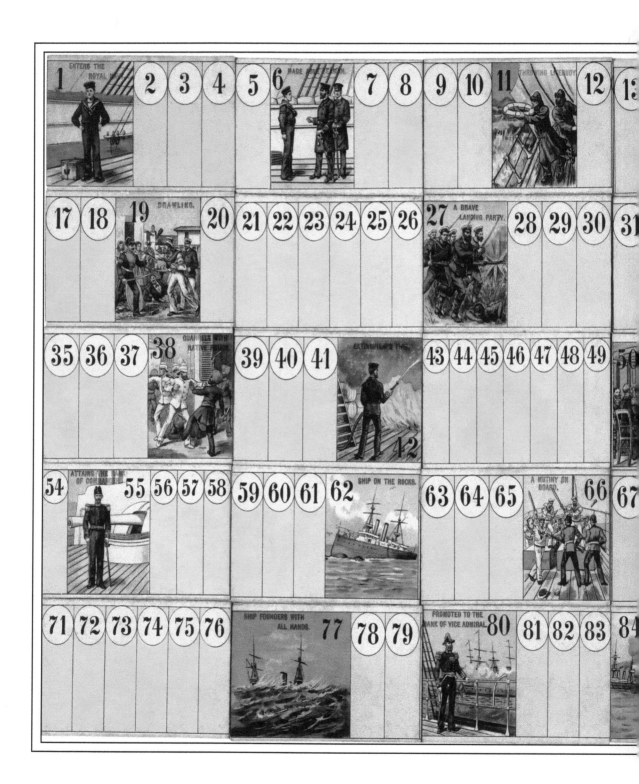

Here we have a board game without a board! Instead, the board is a pack of numbered cards, which players can lay out in their desired track shape. The London-based C W Faulkner & Co. produced a series of games on this model. The first, called Upidee, was themed around a horse race over fences. This particular game maps out an ideal career in the Royal Navy for a sailor-boy, advancing from Able Seaman to Boatswain, and eventually progressing through officer ranks such as Commander, Captain, and Vice-Admiral. The journey is dotted with various naval adventures. For example, saving the Captain from sharks earns a medal and an extra turn. Meanwhile, at space 50, there's a Court-martial where the sailor is tried for being drunk on duty, losing five years' seniority (promotions in the Royal Navy back then were based on years served at a particular rank). However, a grave mistake awaits at space 62, where a navigational error causes the ship to crash into rocks. This error results in the player's dismissal from the service, ending their game. The vibrant chromolithographed images of sailors in uniform make this game particularly engaging.

Boer and Rooinek
Game. Designed
by E G Schlette.
Amsterdam: Koster
Bros.

about 1900

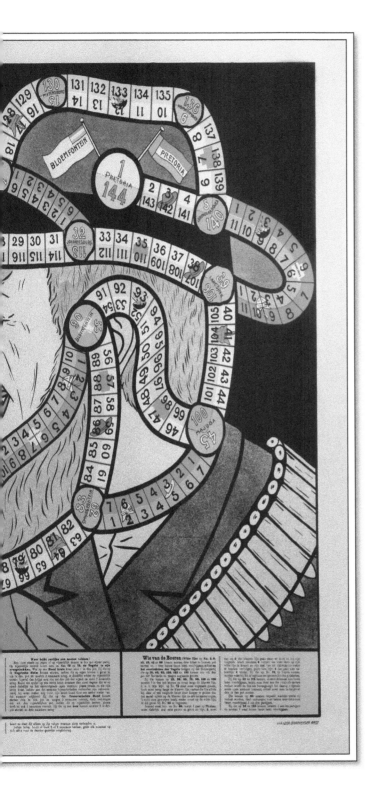

The *Boer and Rooinek Game,* though crudely made, packs a punch with its powerful caricatures. 'Rooinek'—derived from Afrikaans meaning 'Red-neck'—is a disparaging term historically used for English-speaking South Africans. It's believed to originate from the sunburnt necks of British soldiers in South Africa. This game emerged during the Second Boer War (1899-1902), a conflict between the British Empire and two Boer states: the South African Republic and the Orange Free State. Initially, the Boers held the upper hand, securing victories at Colenso, Magersfontein, and Stormberg and besieging places like Ladysmith, Kimberley, and Mafeking (currently known as Mahikeng). The game mirrors these initial triumphs, as depicted by the distressed British soldier juxtaposed with the jubilant Boer. However, as the war progressed, the British deployed massive reinforcements, ensuring their eventual victory. The game features two contrasting numbered tracks. Boers kick off from Pretoria, navigating the white track towards their victory point at Kaapstad (Cape Town), marked as space 144. The Rooineks, on the other hand, traverse the yellow track but in the opposite direction. The red and blue tracks serve as shortcuts for the Rooineks and the Boers, respectively, which they take whenever they encounter a connecting point on their main routes. The game adheres to its unique set of rules.

New Game of Besieging.
Amsterdam: [probably] Vlieger
about 1880

In this unique setup, an older game sheet is displayed in the top left corner of a larger sheet. This larger sheet has added rules and is adorned with vibrant combat scenes. The older sheet can be traced back to around 1860, based on the central image. The primary figure closely resembles King William III, who reigned as the King of the Netherlands and the Grand Duke of Luxembourg from 1849 until he passed away in 1890. The illustration depicts him as the army's commander-in-chief, dressed in the Royal Netherlands Army uniform from the period of 1854-1865. Players roll a pair of dice on the 56-space track. The first move is determined by each player's roll, with the one getting the highest roll becoming the General. As players navigate towards the battlefield, they encounter various challenges illustrated by small images, each with its own set of rules. For instance, upon reaching space 11, showcasing the King, players need to give up ten tokens to secure a premium spot to witness his procession. At space 14, players must wait a round, similar to what's required at space 28, which depicts guard duty. A significant setback awaits at space 52. If you land here, you're identified as a spy disguised as a street musician. Consequently, you're executed in front of the army, and just like the lethal spot in the Goose game, you have to start over.

NIEUW BELEGERINGSPEL.

door elk der medespelenden een overeen te komen getal fishes of penningen in den pot gedaan. Vervolgens wordt overgegaan tot het benoemen van een Generaal, hetgeen door het lot wordt beslist. Hij is zijn adjudant-betaalmeester, den oudste in jaren van het gezelschap. De Generaal speelt het eerst en heeft het recht de door hem geworpen oogen te doen gelden of wel op nieuw te gooien. Een klein ft vervolgens de dobbelsteenen aan zijn rechterbuur, en zoo doet elk op zijnen beurt, tot dat een der manschappen eindelijk het slagveld (No. 56) bereikt, en het spel wint. Op den weg echter naar het slagveld ontmoet men tal van hindernissen, waarvoor de volgende regels gelden: Wie op 3 komt en vermuimt voor den hem passeerenden kapitein te salueeren betaalt zes penningen, en wie op 6 komt vier penningen tot onderhoud van den trommel, doch heeft daarvoor het recht direct tot 12 door te marcheeren. Wie op 8 komt blaast op de trompet en ontvangt daarvoor drie penningen, terwijl hij die op 11 komt zich voor zes penningen eene goede plaats koopt om den Koning te zien passeeren. Wie in de Cachot (14) komt, moet daar overnachten en dus zijn beurt één laten voorbijgaan. Wie op 16 komt ontvangt zes penningen en wie op 20 komt, wordt in de vesting opgesloten, ten zij hij vier penningen losgeld betale. Wie op 23 komt huurt eene veldtent voor den nacht, volgens tarief zes penningen. Wie op 26 komt gebruikt in het Bivouak zijn ontbijt, waarvoor hij 5 penningen verschuldigd is. Wie op 28 komt, lost den schildwacht af en blijft aldaar op zijn post tot hij op zijne beurt verlost wordt. Op 31 gekomen neemt men van de marketenster een glaasje bier voor drie penningen. Wie op 34 komt ontvangt voor elke weg te dragen korf van iederen speler een penning, ze moeten echter naar het slagveld gebracht worden, hetgeen veel tijd kost. Hierdoor heeft hij geen tijd verder te gaan en last zijn beurt drie maal passeeren. Wie op 36 komt betaald voor den aankoop van kruit zes penningen en wie op 39 komt vraagt den weg naar No. 47 om zijn wonden te laten verbinden. Hij betaalt daarvoor vier penningen aan zijnen linker- en rechter nevenman, doch vertrekt dan ook onmiddelijk derwaarts. Wie op 43 komt gaat onmiddelijk terug naar den Koning (No. 11) om hem mede te deelen, dat de Vesting in brand staat, hij ontvangt 12 penningen reisgeld. Wie op 47 komt betaald tot instandhouding van het fonds: het Roode Kruis 8 penningen, doch zijn die van No. 39 derwaarts zijn gewezen hiervan uitgesloten. Wie op 52 komt, wordt als Spion herkend in het gewaad van een orgeldraaier, om voor het front der troepen te worden gefusileerd. Hij begint daarop weder van voren aan. Wie op 56 komt wint het spel en wordt voor het volgende Generaal. Komt men over 56 dan moeten zooveel punten achteruit geteld; tenzij men is overeengekomen, dat dan weder van voren af moet worden geworpen op No. 1 af bijgesteld. Wie in dit geval op No. 1 komt ontvangt van elk rij penningen reisgeld. Achterhalen twee spelers elkaar, dan neemt de eerst op de plaats vertoevende, de plaats in, waar van de andere gekomen is; hij ontvangt daarvoor echter van dezen twee penningen.

125

PREMIE op WARENDORF'S GEÏLLUSTREERDE FAMILIEKALENDER 19

AMST. BOEK- EN STEENDRUKKERIJ, v/h. Ellerman, Harms & Co., Amsterdam.

This impressive game sheet was included as a complimentary addition to Warendorf's *Illustrated Family Calendar* in 1903. The Calendar was released annually, featuring nine captivating novels and sixteen color illustrations. The game sheet seems to depict the Aceh War (1873-1914) in the Dutch East Indies. This conflict was initiated by the Kingdom of the Netherlands with the intention of controlling the Strait of Malacca, a vital trade route between the Malay Peninsula and Sumatra, an Indonesian island. The objective was to safeguard this route from pirates originating from Aceh, located at the island's northern tip. The gameplay rules are straightforward. Players follow a track marked by numbered circles. Landing on a red number means contributing the indicated number of tokens to a central pot, while landing on a blue number lets you take tokens. If you land on a spot marked 'H,' you head to the hospital at space 35 and contribute to a different pot, while an 'A' directs you to the field hospital at space 81. The game's victor earns a medal, referred to as the 'Knight's Cross,' along with the central pot's contents. Meanwhile, the last player remaining in the hospital claims its dedicated pot. Interestingly, the game's artwork was adapted from an earlier 1879 game. Additions include palm trees and a building showcasing an Eastern dome. The 1879 version portrayed the Boer War and wasn't related to the Far East, explaining the respectful representation of the Aceh warriors, depicted in strategic defensive positions.

Asalto. Barcelona: Paluzie
about 1900

*A*salto (which translates to 'Assault') is a two-player strategy game known by various names, including *German Tactics* in this version. To play on the game sheet, you'll need two game pieces of one color to represent the Officers and twenty-four pieces of another color for the Rebels. The two Officers, defending the fortress at the top of the sheet, start on any of the spaces numbered 1 to 9. The Rebels start on the 24 red spaces below the fortress. One player commands the Officers while the other controls the Rebels, each moving one piece per turn, starting with the Rebels.

Rebels can only move forward to any adjacent, unoccupied space along the white lines and are restricted from moving on the black lines. On the other hand, Officers can move in any direction to an adjacent space. Officers can also 'capture' (or remove) a Rebel similarly to the game of Checkers. They jump over the Rebel in any direction, but only if the space immediately after the Rebel is free. This jump has to be linear. Officers can't be captured, nor can they jump over each other.

The Rebels are victorious if they can push both Officers out of the fortress and claim all nine numbered spaces. Conversely, the Officers win if they reduce the Rebel count to the point where the Rebels can't achieve their goal. Dive into the challenge and enjoy the game!

Este juego está dividido en cinco partes.—La parte superior, donde los puntos son numerados, representa la fortaleza que, defendida por 2 soldados solamente, ha de luchar contra las cuatro partes inferiores ocupadas por los sitiadores.—Los 2 soldados sitiados se colocan á voluntad sobre los puntos numerados y los soldados sitiadores se deben colocar sobre los 24 puntos rojos.—Los 24 soldados sitiadores sólo pueden avanzar por las líneas blancas en dirección recta ó diagonal, sin poder retroceder ni seguir las líneas negras.—A cada jugada uno de los soldados adelanta un paso del punto donde está al inmediato si está desocupado.—Los 2 soldados sitiados pueden seguir las líneas blancas ó negras y diagonales lo mismo avanzando que retrocediendo.—A cada jugada uno de los soldados que no sean ocupados.—Estos soldados á cada jugada adelantan un paso, excepto cuando toman un sitiador, lo cual se hace lo mismo que en el juego de Damas, es decir, que se puede tomar cada soldado sitiador detrás del cual se encuentre un punto desocupado; así mismo se pueden tomar varias, avanzando y retrocediendo.—Los 2 soldados sitiados deben procurar siempre poderse retirar á la fortaleza.—Los 24 sitiadores no pueden tomar ninguno de los sitiados; pero si les pueden soplar como en el juego de Damas cuando se descuidan de tomar á uno cualquiera de ellos.—La combinación de este juego consiste en expulsar los 2 defensores fuera de la fortaleza y ocupar los 9 puntos de ella con sitiadores.—Se juega por dos personas alternativamente como en el juego de Damas.—Para peones pueden utilizarse soldados de papel encartonados, recortados y con un pie de madera.

Imprenta Elzeviriana y Librería Camí. S. A. Calle Joaquín Costa. 64 Barcelona

Sports and Leisure: Enjoy the Fun!

Printed race games are so versatile that they can be inspired by nearly any activity, including skating, biking, sledding, and amusement park rides. Such games vividly capture the leisure culture of the 19th century.

As the 19th century progressed, the focus shifted from educational games for children and teenagers to a broader variety that reflected the leisure pursuits of adults. Many of these games aimed to mimic the excitement of high-class entertainment, like cross-country horse races known as steeplechases. Often, the primary thrill of these games was the chance to gamble, mirroring the actual events. The growing middle class, enjoying newfound wealth from the industrial revolution, found themselves with both the time and money to indulge in a variety of recreational activities. Game manufacturers were quick to tap into these trends, creating games that, while not replicating the actual experience, remained

remarkably true to the essence of these activities. For instance, the biking boom in the century's last decade led to numerous bike-themed games worldwide. These games highlighted the various mishaps early bikers might encounter. Given the swift advancements in biking gear, board game designers had to stay on their toes.

Another trend that surged in popularity in the late 19th century was roller skating. This fad even inspired the term 'rinkomania' to capture the sheer excitement it evoked among its enthusiasts. Advances in skate design caused roller skating to gain massive traction in Europe as the century drew to a close. Despite the accidents and embarrassments illustrated in 'The Skating Rink,' a dynamic game featured at the start of this book, the sport soared in popularity. In this game, played on two tracks, if the teams collide at a crossover, they both have a 'wipeout' and have to restart the game. What's truly captivating about the game, however, is the rich tapestry of its social backdrop – from the range of accidents and ensuing reactions to the diverse attire sported by individuals from all walks of life. Right from its inception, roller skating offered a space for youngsters of both genders to mingle, breaking away from restrictive norms – marking a subtle yet pivotal shift in the sexual revolution.

Adding to these athletic recreations were the mechanized rides at amusement parks. Some targeted younger children, while others, like the Great Wheel at the 1900 Paris Expo, catered to a broader demographic. These innovations, too, were immortalized in the form of board games. 'The Game of the Flower Parade' stands as a testament to how societal events were adapted into game themes, immortalizing remarkable royal ceremonies. In stark contrast, the 'Saint Nicholas Game'

transports players to a typical Dutch household, capturing the enchantment of a night dedicated to gifting and feasting in the Netherlands.

Creativity was also evident in adapting traditional games for modern leisure. Take 'Snakes and Ladders' for instance – though introduced to Europe in the late 19th century, it traces its roots back to ancient morality-based games from places like India, Nepal, and Tibet, possibly going back as far as the 13th century. In these ancestral versions, players would climb towards Vishnu or Nirvana, with virtues propelling them forward and vices causing setbacks via snakes. A streamlined version emerged in England by 1892, fast becoming a kids' favorite. While mainland Europe didn't fully embrace the classic 'Snakes and Ladders,' it did spawn variations, including ones themed around circuses or, as depicted in this game, sledding on ice.

The Steeplechase Game. Paris: Rousseau
about 1880

'*The Steeplechase' Game* depicts a horse race that hurdles over fences, hedges, and ditches. The unfolding board is sizable, extending to about 28.7 x 18.9 inches, and boasts colorful lithography, further enhanced by hand-colored details. This game likely came in an impressive box containing hand-painted, metal-cast model horses, accompanied by a collection of fences and other obstacles to adorn the track. Crafted in Paris for the English audience, this game is of impeccable quality. However, a quick glance at the instructions, centered on the board, reveals some English language errors. This game involves wagers. Participants could choose multiple horses, but for every additional horse after the first, they'd owe one-and-a-half times the initial wager. Landing on space 57 shows a horse tumbling over a fence – such a horse would need to start over without further penalty. However, space 84, representing the water jump, is more penalizing – a horse landing here starts over and owes an additional stake. Spaces marked with a circled number act as pauses, causing the horse to backtrack. Similar rules apply to hurdles, barriers, and ditches. Players use two dice for the game, but they can opt for four dice to expedite the game, especially towards the conclusion. Given the potential frequency of stake exchanges, it's clear why money might change hands rapidly. Interestingly, it seems the game creators doubted the perfection of their rules. In the end, they suggest players can 'set their own rules.'

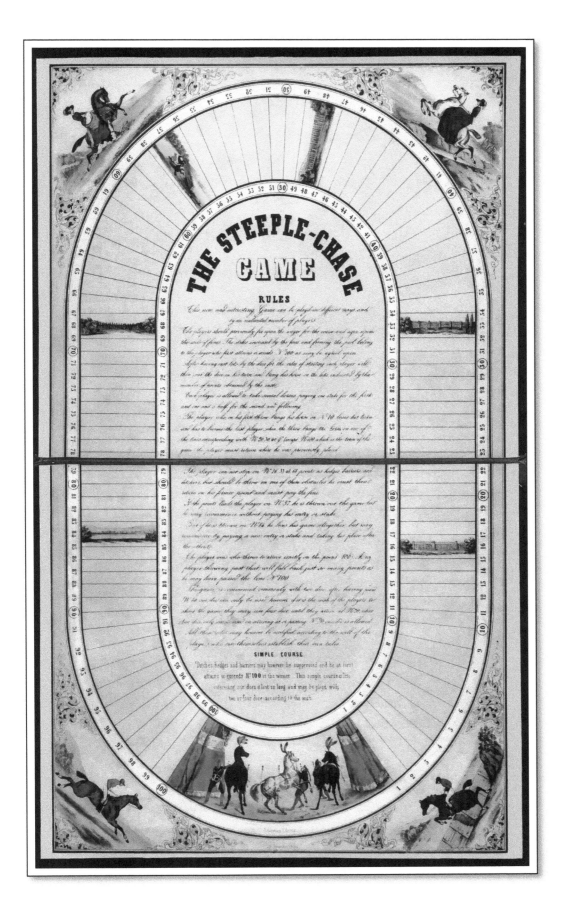

THE STEEPLE-CHASE GAME

RULES

This new and interesting Game can be played in different ways and by an unlimited number of players

The players should previously fix upon the wager for the course and agree upon the value of fines. The stakes received by the first and forming the pool belong to the player who first attains or sounds N° 100 as may be agreed upon

After having cast lots by the dice for the order of starting each player will then cast the dice in his turn and bring his horse on the line indicated by the number of points obtained by the cast.

Each player is allowed to take several horses paying one stake for the first and one and a half for the second and following

The player who on his first throw brings his horse on N° 10 loses his stake and has to become the last player when the throw brings the Green on one of the lines corresponding with N° 20, 30, 40 & (except N° 100 which is the term of the game) the player must return where he was previously placed

The player can not stop on N° 16, 33 & 68 points as hedges barriers and ditches but should he throw on one of these obstacles he must then return on his former point and must pay the fine

If the points lands the player on N° 57 he is thrown over the game but may commence without paying his entry or stake

But if he is thrown on N° 84 he loses his game altogether but may commence by paying a new entry or stake and taking his place after the others

The player wins who throws to attain exactly on the point 100. Any player throwing past that will fall back just so many points as he may have passed the line N° 100

The game is commenced commonly with two dice after having past N° 80, one die can only be used however & it is the wish of the players to shorten the game they may use four dice until they attain at N° 80, when two dice only may be used on attaining at or passing N° 80 no die is allowed

All these rules may however be modified according to the will of the players each one themselves establish their own rules

SIMPLE COURSE

Ditches hedges and barriers may however be suppressed and he at first attains or exceeds N° 100 is the winner. This simple course is less interesting nor does it last so long and may be played with two or four dice according to the wish

Saint Nicholas Game. Amsterdam: Vlieger about 1890

In the Netherlands, children eagerly await *Sinterklaas* or *Sint-Nicolaas*, a legendary figure inspired by Saint Nicholas, the children's patron saint. Every year, the eve before Saint Nicholas' Day on December 6th is marked by gift-giving. *Sinterklaas* is the main inspiration behind our *Santa Claus*. At the heart of the decoration, the saint is portrayed distributing gifts with the help of *Zwarte Piet* (Black Peter), traditionally considered a Moor from Spain. This game ingeniously tweaks the classic 'Game of Goose' to capture the joyous traditions of the evening. One prevalent custom is placing presents in kids' boots or shoes. In the game, the favorable positions, marked with numbers like 9, 18, 27, and so on, are aptly symbolized. Risky spaces are child-friendly interpretations: the *Inn* transforms into the Toy Store, where a payment means skipping a turn, and the ominous *Death* space turns into Black Peter's sack, depicting a mischievous child caught and carried away. The initial roll of nine has unique rules, differing for boys and girls. Depending on the specifics of the roll, players might find themselves promised in marriage to either a fetching lady/gentleman on spaces 25/26 or a less appealing older individual on spaces 51/53.

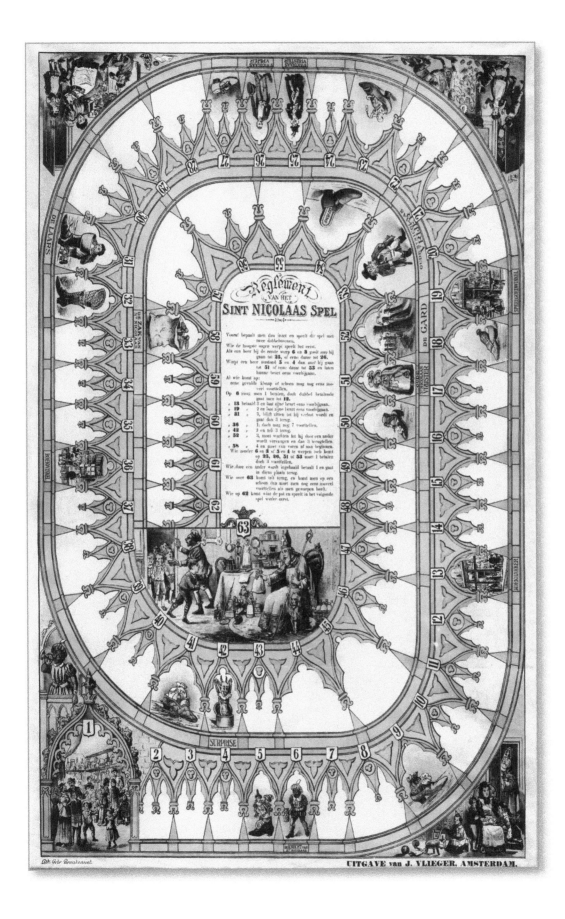

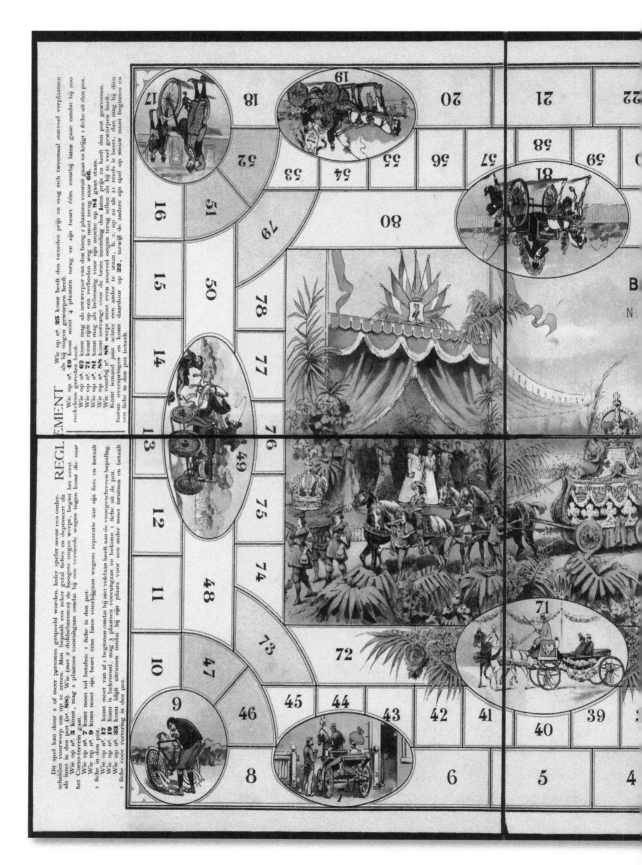

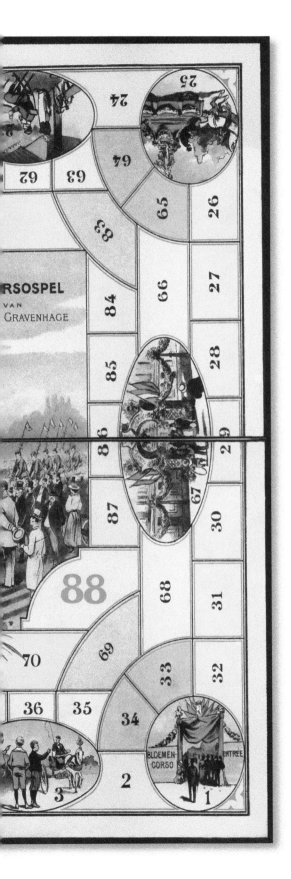

Flower parades are a cherished tradition in the Netherlands, taking place in the spring throughout the bulb-growing region. The parade depicted in this game, held in The Hague, commemorates a notable event: the inauguration of Queen Wilhelmina. Born in 1880, she ascended to the throne as the Queen of the Netherlands following King William III's demise in 1890. However, her mother served as regent until 1898 when Wilhelmina reached an age suitable for her official coronation. This game illustrates her observing the parade from a draped platform, flanked by her mother and other royal family members. A float, pulled by four horses and adorned in the royal orange hue, topped with a floral crown, is evidently the parade's winner. The game's track, spanning 88 spaces, showcases various episodes encountered en route to the parade. The game vividly captures the Dutch fervor for cycling as a mode of transportation, though with its fair share of challenges. On space 9, players halt a turn to mend a bicycle. Space 23 offers a pitstop, allowing for a refreshment and a tobacco pipe puff, but players must pause until another participant comes to replace them. Riding in a wagon isn't devoid of setbacks either: on space 49, your wagon has struck a pedestrian, forcing you to backtrack four spaces and forfeit a turn due to reckless driving. On the flip side, landing on space 25 signifies clinching the second prize for your float, doubling your points. Distinctively, if a roll positions you directly behind another player, you leap over them, compelling them to restart the game.

Carousel Game.
Amsterdam: Jos. Vas Dias
1889

In addition to offering a delightful depiction of kids reveling in a fairground ride, the *Carousel* game is strikingly novel. One distinct feature initiates the game with players vying to become the *pachter*, or the man who leases the carousel. He's depicted standing on the right, clutching his money pouch. This figure collects one token from any player landing on the red numbers. Tokens amassed are awarded to the player who placed the highest bid at the onset. The tokens from that initial bid contribute to the winner's pot, located at the center's number seven. This pot grows as each player contributes a token during every turn. Another inventive aspect is the use of two dice, whose values are multiplied to dictate the move, contrasting the typical addition approach. Consequently, overshooting the winning space, labeled 37, becomes quite plausible. Surplus points redirect players to the beginning, a deviation from the Goose game's backtrack system. This setup embodies the game's cyclical nature, akin to a real carousel. Additionally, if one player's token intersects with another's, the affected player restarts. Not only does this game enhance kids' mathematical skills, but it also hones their betting acumen, necessitating foresight about the game's duration. The *pachter* significantly benefits from extended play. Whether this game serves as an apt primer for real-world challenges is a matter of perspective.

Figure · S. WARENDORF Jr. Amsterdam.

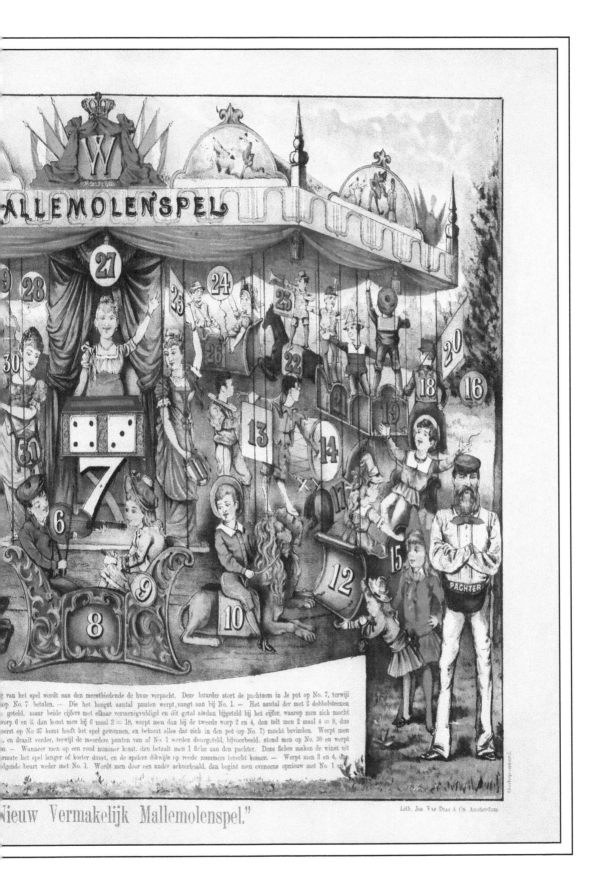

Game of the Giant Wheel of Paris.
Paris: Fabrique S. C.
1900

The Giant Wheel, a marvel of its time, was built for the *Exposition Universelle* in Paris in 1899 to celebrate achievements of the previous century and look forward to the next. Towering at 106 meters, it dwarfed the original Chicago Ferris Wheel from 1883. Inspired by its design, a board game was crafted. Instead of the traditional 63 spaces of the Goose game, the game incorporated 40 spaces, representing the wheel's carriages. The game retained elements of the Goose game, including various hazards, although the positioning of certain spaces was altered. The game also beautifully illustrated iconic Paris landmarks, such as the Eiffel Tower, enhancing the gaming experience.

Cycle Sport Game. Amsterdam: Vlieger

1891

The Cycle Sport Game gives a glimpse into the evolution of cycling in 1891. It features diverse cycles, from the treacherous 'penny-farthing' to various trikes, and showcases the different headgear of the era. The game incorporates elements of the classic Goose game but introduces a twist with two tracks for two teams: red and blue. An initial dice throw can earn a player significant advancements. The game has unique spaces, such as the water cycle, inspired by the real Pinkert Navigating Tricycle, an ambitious invention of the time.

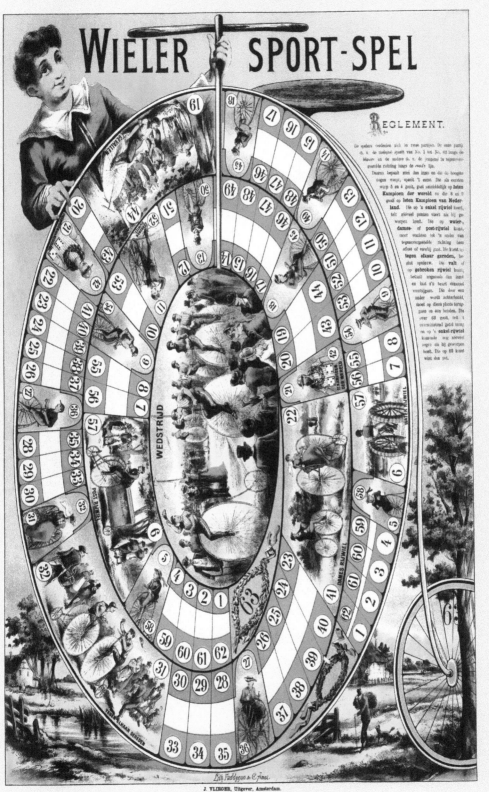

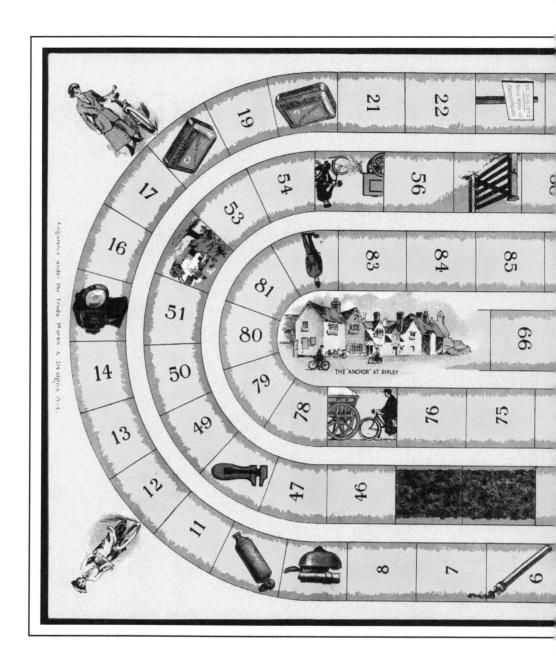

Wheeling. London: Jaques

1900

By the turn of the 20th century, bike technology had made significant strides, especially with the introduction of the 'safety bicycle.' Biking became a popular weekend activity for many. A hot spot for bikers from London was The Anchor, a pub in Ripley, a Surrey village located on the way to Portsmouth, about 22 miles southwest of London. The game *Wheeling* centers

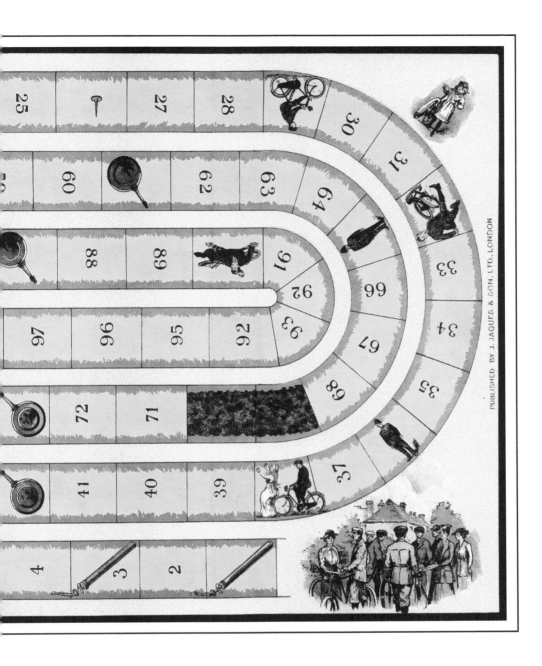

PUBLISHED BY J. JAQUES & SON, LTD, LONDON

around this scenic journey, culminating at The Anchor as the final destination. To begin, players must roll a 1, 3, or 6 on a single die to 'pump up their tires'; after that, they roll two dice. Although the game doesn't seem directly inspired by the Game of the Goose, it bears similarities like a consistent series of beneficial spots, for example, every oil can, which lets the player advance an extra five spaces. In the game's early stages, players can earn 'tickets' (cards that come with the game) for accessories like a bell, whistle, pneumatic outfit, or lamp. These tickets can later protect the player from setbacks, such as at space 26 (a sharp tack). Without a pneumatic outfit ticket, a player would have to backtrack to space 10 to acquire one. However, there's a game-ending hazard at space 90: if a player lands there, they 'break' their bike and are out of the game.

On the Ice. Paris: Saussine about 1900

'Sur la Glace' (On the Ice) is a beautifully designed chromolithograph game created by Saussine, a renowned French game manufacturer that operated from the 1860s to the 1960s. Known for their original and appealing designs, Saussine targeted both the French and international markets, often providing rules in both French and English and keeping the game board free of text. 'Sur la Glace' is reminiscent of the English game *Snakes and Ladders*, with toboggan tracks serving as the game's 'ladders.' The game board consists of 100 spaces set on a zigzag rectangular track. However, it does differ from its predecessor, particularly lacking the long descents near the end, which could have added extra excitement to the game, similar to the *death* space in the Game of the Goose. The game's design prioritizes visual balance over such unexpected twists.

Satire and Polemic: Games with a Bite!

These games are not for children. The French had a particular fondness for games based on political intrigues like the Dreyfus case, but other countries also enjoyed these witty adult pursuits.

Most of the games in this chapter come from France, where satirical and polemical games have a long history, dating back to the end of the 17th century when a game satirizing the complexities and frustrations of the legal system was introduced. That game's endpoint was the workhouse, a result of the crippling costs and reversals of taking a legal case. Unlike the Game of the Goose, this one had no beneficial spaces at all.

This chapter kicks off with a game detailing the French Revolution, filled with satirical references to the Ancien Régime that had

been toppled. Then, we encounter a game with a hidden agenda: to endorse the Bourbon monarchy's restoration. Every major shift in France's turbulent 19th-century history spawned board games with potent political content. For instance, the transition to the Third Republic in 1870 after the Second Empire's downfall, led to the intricate Parliamentary Game of the Goose. This game, bursting with satire, ridiculed parliamentary customs even before the new order was solidly in place. The Game of Laws, launched around the same time in the satirical journal Charivari, was similar but focused on condemning Napoleon III's Second Empire.

Europe's 19th century wasn't just about France; it witnessed political shifts elsewhere too. Italy's unification inspired the game,

'Italy in the Nineteenth Century.' Published in a satirical magazine, this game exudes a sense of patriotism and hope for a unified Italy, looking back fondly at influential figures who championed the revolutionary cause. In France, the Dreyfus affair ignited political debates at the century's turn. In 1894, Captain Alfred Dreyfus, a young Jewish artillery officer, was wrongfully convicted of treason. He spent nearly five years imprisoned on Devil's Island before his innocence was recognized. This polarizing event inspired the 1898 game, 'The Dreyfus Affair and the Truth,' which mocked the injustice and duplicity of those in power.

The 'Humbert affair' also birthed a contentious game. Thérèse Humbert, once a peasant girl, shared an incredible tale. She claimed to have helped an ailing wealthy American on a train in 1879. In return, he promised her a substantial inheritance. Leveraging this story, she borrowed vast amounts of money, leading a luxurious life in Paris for nearly two decades. The Game of the Rabbit of La Grande Therese not only captures her meteoric rise and subsequent fall but also lampoons the gullible individuals, some of whom held high-ranking positions, she fooled.

In England, political chaos ensued as well – the focal point being the suffragette movement, fighting for women's voting rights. The game 'Pank-a-Squith' stands out as a unique English political board game. Set against the suffragette movement's signature colors of purple and green, it depicts the suffragettes' fierce yet futile battle. It wasn't until after World War I that women in England secured the right to vote.

Game of the French Revolution.
Paris: publisher unknown
1790

This game celebrates the principles and accomplishments of the French Revolution. Every square features an illustration, chronicling the initial months of the Revolution, starting with the Storming of the Bastille on July 14, 1789, and culminating at the winning space, number 63, showcasing the National Assembly at the Palladium of Liberty. The positive *Goose* squares laud the abolition of the *Parlements*. Established in medieval times, these law courts had stymied reforms, especially those intending to tax the nobility more. As strongholds of resistance and privilege, they were swiftly dismantled by the Revolution. The game portrays them with humorous illustrations of geese dressed as attorneys, labeled in the rules as oies *bridées*, translating to 'nincompoops.' The game's hazard spaces also receive a satirical makeover. For instance, the maze at square 42 depicts the Châtelet of Paris, a prominent law court, suggesting that justice there is elusive. Square 58 recounts the demise of Delaunay, Foulon, Berthier, and others. The Marquis de Launay, the Bastille's Governor, faced mob lynching after its siege. Foulon, the Finance Controller appointed in 1789, was widely detested. He attempted to flee Paris but was apprehended and executed by the populace alongside his son-in-law, Berthier. The game illustrates his beheaded likeness with hay stuffed in his mouth, a nod to his ill-advised remark that the famished should resort to hay.

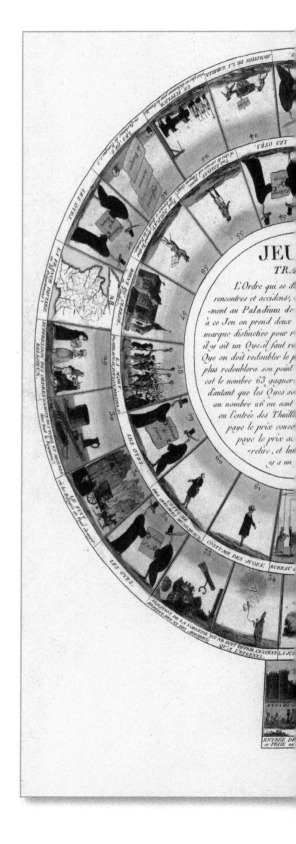

LA RÉVOLUTION FRANÇAISE,
PLAN DU JEU D'OYE RENOUVELE DES GRECS.

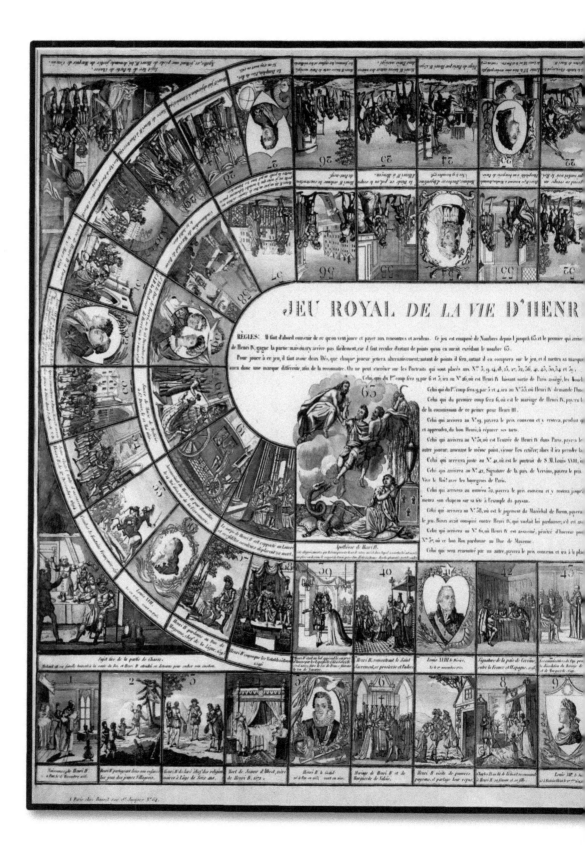

JEU ROYAL DE LA VIE D'HENR[...]

Royal Game of the Life of Henri IV.
Paris: Basset
1815

The *Royal Game of the Life of Henri IV* seemingly provides a direct historical portrayal of this beloved king, who's credited with desiring to ensure every French citizen had 'a chicken in the pot.' The game illustrates moments from Henri's life, from his 1553 birth to his assassination represented on square 61. The ultimate winning square, 63, portrays his ascension to heaven, as painted by Rubens. However, beneath the surface, this game carries a nuanced political undertone. It lauds the Bourbon Restorations, which saw Louis XVIII ascend the French throne post-Napoleon. The game, reminiscent of the classic Goose format, displays all beneficial spaces with the newly installed royal lineage. The embedded message is that Henri's esteemed reputation will somehow bless the Restoration. A distinct rule is attached to square 41, depicting Louis XVIII: players are directed to 'dine with Henri IV' at square 55. This image captures Henri before a sizable fireplace where a turkey roasts for his meal. A popular, albeit possibly apocryphal, tale claims that prior to the Battle of Ivry, Henri, incognito, visited an officer's residence in Alençon. Unrecognized by the officer's wife and lacking a meal for him, she borrowed a turkey from a neighbor. This neighbor, known for his wit, entertained Henri during dinner, leading the king to bestow nobility upon him, symbolized by a coat of arms featuring a roasting turkey.

Parliamentary
Game of the Goose.
Paris:
Vancortenberghen
1871

The expansive and striking *Parliamentary Game of the Goose* features portraits of prominent French politicians of the time, alongside humorous sketches. This unique game sets the 'left' against the 'right': each faction plays on its own 50-space track. The goal for the 'left' is to reach the last space, labeled *change of government*, before the 'right' lands on their end space, titled *vote of confidence*. The game mirrors the French legislative assembly, shaped like a semicircle split in half, reminiscent of the Chamber. The middle showcases a podium with the customary glass of sugar-water for orators, and beneath it, the President's seat with a bell to oversee debates. It appears the assembly was often boisterous, filled with murmurs, whistles, objections, loud laughter, and numerous disruptions. The game rules, differing for each side, seem either incomplete or challenging to discern in gameplay terms. This suggests the game might've been designed more for comedic enjoyment than serious play.

JEU DE LOIS.

Pour jouer à ce jeu, il faut deux dés que chacun des joueurs jette à son tour : on additionne le nombre de points donné par les et l'on va à la case portant le chiffre correspondant au nombre indiqué sur les dés. Mais avant d'arriver au but nombre d'obstacles sent devant les joueurs dont la plus grande chance est de tomber sur une des Lois. Ces Lois sont au nombre de 13, et portent le nu 9, 11, 18, 23, 27, 32, 36, 41, 45, 50, 54 et 59. Chaque fois que vous seignez un de ces numéros, vous avancez vers le but d' points que vous en avez eu pour arriver à ce numéro.

Le joueur qui arrive au n° 2, Irrèche d'Émile, est renvoyé au 22, la librairie d'Ille, où il paie une mise pour frais d'achats.

Le N° 3 — les Invalides — mè au 31, l'Académie, où vous restez jusqu'à ce que les autres joueurs aient dépassé ce point.

N° 6. — Jules Favre vous enie vous noyer dans la Fontaine des Larmes, n° 1.

N° 7. — Le Plébiscite vous enie au 11, à Sedan, où vous restez jusqu'à ce que des joueurs soit arrive au 58 Bismark.

N° 10. — Faidherbe mène au l'écritoire militaire.

N° 13. — L'Empire vous envoie au 17, le casse-tête; vous payez et allez vous reposer au 32, la prison, où vous restez jusqu'à ce qu'un autre prenne votre place.

N° 19. — Chambord vous envoie au 8, dans les toiles d'araignées, où vous restez dix coups sans jouer.

N° 33. — Le Prussien vous enie au magasin de pendules n° 21, où vous payez une mise.

N° 34. — L'Académie vous renvoie au 3, les Invalides.

N° 35. — Bazaine vous envoie Metz, n° 4, où vous restez jusqu'à ce qu'un de joueurs soit atteint le n° 57, l'armistice.

N° 31. — Trochu. On paie et on sort plus.

N° 37. — Pouyer-Quertier vous porte au n° 49, l'Évacuation.

N° 38. — Damas fils vous fait lancer au n° 39, à une Feuille de vigne.

N° 30. — La Censure vous envoie au loh. Vous payez deux mises d'amende comme il est dit plus haut.

N° 40. — Basile vous renvoi au n° 16, l'

N° 28. — L'Exorcisme, vous porte a Gambetta sortant d'un bénitier.

N° 42. — Veuillot vous envoie au n° 3 sarée, où vous payez.

N° 44. — La Loi. / Vous payez troi allez au n° 11.
N° 46. — Les Cocottes. / vous subissez ci-dessous écrit

N° 47. — Ducrot vous envoie au 25, le n° 30, l'école.

N° 48. — Le suffrage universel vous
N° 51. — Fusion. Vous envoie au 26 rinthe.

N° 53. — Thiers. Arrivé à ce num avez droit de retirer votre mise.

N° 55. — La Paire de sabots vous n° 7, le Plébiscite.

N° 56. — Le départ du numéraire ro an 29, où vous payez pour le change.

N° 58. — Bismark. Vous payez cinq c'est à recommencer.

N° 60. — Quand vous arrivez à 60 l'est représenté le prince Napoléon rega panoplie, vous reculez si vivement, quo vous arrêtez au n° 7.

N° 62. — La Commune, derrière ce but, vous fait reculer d'autant de points en avez eu pour y arriver

N° 63. — La République gagne.

RÉPUBLIQUE

G. La Joss

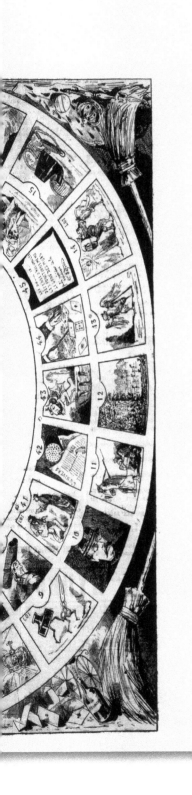

The *Game of Laws* satirizes the Second Empire, which collapsed with Napoleon III's downfall. The game's tone is hinted in the top left corner: it displays various masks, allowing politicians to conceal their real intentions, paired with a 'phrase book of fancy terms for top officials.' All are being cleared out by a large broom. Proposed laws for the forthcoming administration are highlighted on the Goose squares. A particular disdain is evident for Otto von Bismarck, the German Empire's Chancellor from 1871. He played a pivotal role in initiating the Franco-Prussian war in 1870, where France faced significant setbacks. Bismarck's 'prize' is his depiction on the game's *death* space. The former emperor, Napoleon III, doesn't fare much better – his figure stands on square 60, donned in a sharp uniform. The game rule humorously states: 'upon landing here, you'll recoil so fast that you won't halt until reaching square number 1.' The

Commune – a radical leftist regime established after the March 1871 revolt of Parisian workers and the National Guard – also faces criticism. It's represented by a petrol-filled container on square 62, alluding to the molotov cocktails during the uprisings. Only the Republic gets a nod of approval, evident on the winning space.

Italy in the 19th Century.
Milan: La Cicala Politica
1861

A pivotal moment in Italy's unification was marked by the release of a patriotic variant of the Game of the Goose on February 25, 1861. This was showcased in a page inserted in the satirical magazine, *La Cicala Politica*, based in Milan. The game, titled *Italy in the 19th Century, or the Newest Game of the Goose*, highlights individuals believed to be crucial in driving political transformation. These 'notable Italians' function as goose spaces, where players can double the number they roll. Featured are writers like Giacomo Leopardi and Ugo Foscolo, alongside generals including Napoleon Bonaparte and Guglielmo Pepe. The Nationalist Bandiera brothers, Attilio and Emilio, whose sacrifice in 1844 inspired subsequent revolts, are also honored. Additionally, key figures Vittorio Emmanuele II and Count Cavour are spotlighted, though Mazzini is conspicuously absent. Spaces along the track are marked by emblematic images, such as the Papal Slipper between spaces 52 and 53, labeled 'agreement.' The jail space showcases the Castle of Spielberg, a notorious prison where many Carbonari (rebels) were detained by the Austro-Hungarian authority. The space corresponding to 'death' in the game is symbolized by 'Diplomacy' at number 46, prompting players to restart. At the victory square, Garibaldi and Victor Emmanuel stand proudly, saluting a flag bearing the motto: 'Italy for the Italians.'

L'ITALIA DEL SECOLO DECIMONONO
OSSIA
IL NUOVISSIMO GIUOCO DELL' OCA
INVENTATO DA PUFF E DISEGNATO DA DON CICCIO.

160

The Dreyfus Affair and the Truth.
Paris: L'Aurore
1898

*T*he *Dreyfus Affair and the Truth* was a board game launched in 1898 by the French magazine *L'Aurore*, spotlighting the injustices surrounding the Dreyfus Affair. This game offers a twist on the traditional Game of the Goose, with the character of 'Truth' taking the place of the geese. The ultimate goal is to land on square 63, which depicts 'the bare truth.' Spaces 24 and 21 feature caricatures of the Court President who presided over Dreyfus's trial, as well as the District Attorney. Square 52 displays the Cherche-Midi military jail in Paris, where Dreyfus was held captive in 1894. Square 31 portrays the Mont Valérien prison, where Hubert-Joseph Henry, a Lieutenant-Colonel in military intelligence, was detained in 1898. He was arrested for fabricating evidence against Dreyfus and eventually took his own life with a razor blade, taking his secret with him. The actual traitor turned out to be Major Ferdinand Esterhazy. He deceitfully asserted that an elusive 'veiled woman' handed him a photograph of a paper that allegedly 'proved' Dreyfus's wrongdoing. The death square, number 58, illustrates the fictional demise of the veiled woman, a character wholly concocted by Esterhazy. The game's comical illustrations amplify the satire, as seen in square 42: the Military General Staff's office is depicted with two officers in a heated argument, papers scattering everywhere.

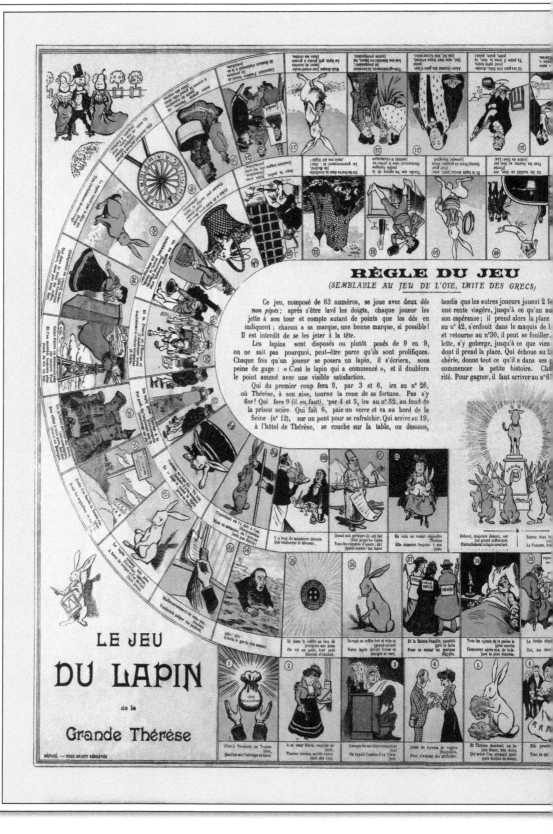

RÈGLE DU JEU
(SEMBLABLE AU JEU DE L'OIE, IMITÉ DES GRECS,)

Ce jeu, composé de 63 numéros, se joue avec deux dés *non pipés*; après s'être lavé les doigts, chaque joueur les jette à son tour et compte autant de points que les dés en indiquent; chacun a sa marque, une bonne marque, si possible! Il est interdit de se les jeter à la tête.

Les lapins sont disposés ou plutôt posés de 9 en 9, on ne sait pas pourquoi, peut-être parce qu'ils sont prolifiques. Chaque fois qu'un joueur se posera un lapin, il s'écriera, sous peine de gage : « C'est le lapin qui a commencé », et il doublera le point amené avec une visible satisfaction.

Qui du premier coup fera 9, par 3 et 6, ira au n° 26, où Thérèse, à son aise, tourne la roue de sa fortune. Pas s'y fier! Qui fera 9 (il en faut), par 4 et 5, ira au n° 52, au fond de la prison noire. Qui fait 6, paie un verre et va au bord de la Seine (n° 12), sur un pont pour se rafraîchir. Qui arrive au 19, à l'hôtel de Thérèse, se couche sur la table, ou dessous,

tandis que les autres joueurs jouent 2 f... une rente viagère, jusqu'à ce qu'un au... son espérance; il prend alors la place... au n° 42, s'enfouit dans le maquis de l... et retourne au n°30, il peut se fouiller... lette, s'y goberge, jusqu'à ce que vien... dont il prend la place. Qui échoue au t... chérie, donne tout ce qu'il a dans ses p... commencer la petite histoire. Ch... rité. Pour gagner, il faut arriver au n°6...

LE JEU
DU LAPIN
de la
Grande Thérèse

LE JEU DU LAPIN

Game of the Rabbit of La Grande
Thérèse. Sceaux: Charaire

1901

The *Game of the Rabbit of La Grande Thérèse* is richly illustrated in a cartoon style, crafted by Fernand Fau, a renowned French illustrator. His artwork depicts the intriguing tale of Thérèse Humbert and her elaborate scam. The game's instructions humorously mention that players should use two dice, but without any dots on them. Rabbits, which pop up on every ninth square, function as the Goose spaces. The significance of the rabbits might puzzle some, but in French jargon from that time, if someone ended up on the losing side of a deal, they were said to 'have bought the rabbit.' This expression is rooted in an old tale about a person who mistakenly sold a cat as if it were a rabbit. However, the game features a rabbit that changes shades quite dramatically. By square 32, it's turned yellow, seemingly dreaming of wealth, and it starts to multiply rapidly. The 'death' square, number 58, illustrates the rabbit trapped under a judge's cap, referencing Thérèse's eventual legal downfall, where she was handed a five-year sentence, including hard labor. The concluding square, 63, showcases multi-colored rabbits dancing around a statue of the Golden Calf, with the label 'Panama.' This alludes to a prior scandal in 1892 when several officials from the French Government accepted kickbacks to overlook the financial pitfalls of the Panama Canal Company. The game humorously criticizes the naivety and avarice of those duped by Thérèse's ruse.

Pank-a-Squith.

Manchester: Women's Social

and Political Union

about 1909

*P*ank-a-Squith gets its title from two prominent political figures of Edwardian England: the suffragette leader Emmeline Pankhurst (1858-1928) and Herbert Asquith, the Prime Minister from 1908 to 1916. The spiral game path depicts the hurdles faced by Mrs. Pankhurst and her allies in their aggressive campaign for women's suffrage, culminating in the ultimate goal at square 50: the Houses of Parliament. The game is likely from around 1909, based on its references. For instance, square 25 alludes to a protest at the Houses of Parliament on June 29, 1909, by members of the Women's Social and Political Union (WSPU), a women-exclusive political group pushing for women's voting rights in the UK. Additionally, square 43 mentions the force-feeding of hunger strikers, a policy introduced that same year. *Pank-a-Squith* was produced by an unidentified German manufacturer to support fundraising for the WSPU. The creator seems to have been unfamiliar with some English terms; for example, square 20 labels the Prime Minister's residence as 'Dowing Street' instead of the correct 'Downing Street.' This German influence might explain why the game's intricate rules are reminiscent of the Game of the Goose, although there isn't a consistent set of beneficial squares. Square 32, representing Holloway Prison (where many suffragettes were incarcerated), serves as a *death* square, meaning players must start over. Square 25 commemorates the courageous delegation on June 29th when Mrs. Pankhurst led eight women to Parliament intending to hand a petition to Mr. Asquith. After he declined to meet them, Mrs. Pankhurst assaulted a police officer. Outside of Parliament, numerous suffragettes clashed with the police, leading to widespread window-breaking. The aftermath saw 107 women and eight men taken into custody.

Advertising and Promotion: Games with a Message

Towards the end of the nineteenth century, color printing became affordable enough that giveaway advertising games were cost-effective. The Dutch likely pioneered this, promoting drinking chocolate, with the French not far behind.

One of the earliest examples of promotional games might have been the 'flyers' certain French newspapers and magazines produced during the Paris Exposition Universelle in 1867, drumming up excitement for this major global event. Proper advertising games started surfacing in the 1880s. One of the first was a savvy adaptation of a Game of the Tramway to market the drinking chocolate from the Dutch company, Van Houten. All they did was incorporate their slogan into an existing print, eliminating the need for a new design. This approach seemed effective because the company soon launched an extensive advertising initiative using specially crafted game sheets in vibrant colors, available in both Dutch and French, targeting a broad European audience.

By the Paris Exposition Universelle in 1889, the advertising approach using the Game of the Goose had evolved significantly in its sophistication. For instance, the French company Jumeau used this strategy to market their high-end dolls, stressing their superiority over the cheaper German imports. They distributed an eye-catching game sheet, which showcased the newly built Eiffel Tower, for free. It was meant 'to be mounted on cardboard and treasured as a memento of the exhibit.'

That same year, the Parisian newspaper, Le Figaro, released an impressive four-page political insert leading up to the French general elections. Every party vying for victory was represented: Republicans, Monarchists, Bonapartists, and as highlighted in this chapter, the Boulangists. They rallied behind 'Le Général,' Georges Ernest Jean-Marie Boulanger (1837–1891). This French general and politician, boasting an impressive military career, reached peak popularity among the working class in January 1889. Many believed he was on the brink of initiating a coup d'état.

However, Boulanger hesitated, and his formidable opponents seized this opportunity. His political endeavors became the subject of scrutiny, leading the French government to issue an arrest warrant. Before they could apprehend him, Boulanger escaped to Brussels and later, London. Following his departure, his support dwindled, his faction suffered a defeat in the elections, and in 1891, he tragically ended his life at the gravesite of his dear mistress in a Brussels graveyard.

As games became a more common advertising medium, designers started incorporating more product details. An especially notable instance was the Game of La Couronne Gas Mantles, which showcased a now nearly obsolete technology, but which, in the late nineteenth century, played a pivotal role in enhancing both home and street illumination.

Some designers cleverly integrated the product into the game rules, as seen in the Ferro-China game. Here, certain dice rolls would suggest the player bolster themselves with a swig of this formerly renowned Italian medicinal tonic digestif – a spirited blend infused with iron and extracts from the bark of the cinchona genus plants (known as 'china' in Italian), rich in quinine and other therapeutic alkaloids.

In another creative twist, sheer imagination drove the game released by the Parisian department store, Galeries Lafayette, in 1906. Capitalizing on the widespread fascination with the emerging world of aviation, the game illustrated an airplane departing from the store's rooftop, soaring over Parisian landmarks, then embarking on a global expedition. This aircraft then darted from Earth, navigating outer space and the Sun, only to safely land back on the same rooftop.

In the Carillon de Flandres game, which promoted chicory as a coffee alternative, the primary draw was its appeal to children. This was achieved by adorning the game path with illustrations of animals, birds, and whimsical characters from the commedia dell'arte. A more direct appeal to the younger audience is evident in this chapter's concluding example, the Game of Nutrix Dwarves. Here, biscuits unlock a fairy tale adventure. This segues into the twentieth century, underscoring how games have been instrumental in shaping advanced marketing strategies.

Game of the Paris Exhibition. Paris: La Vie Parisienne 1867

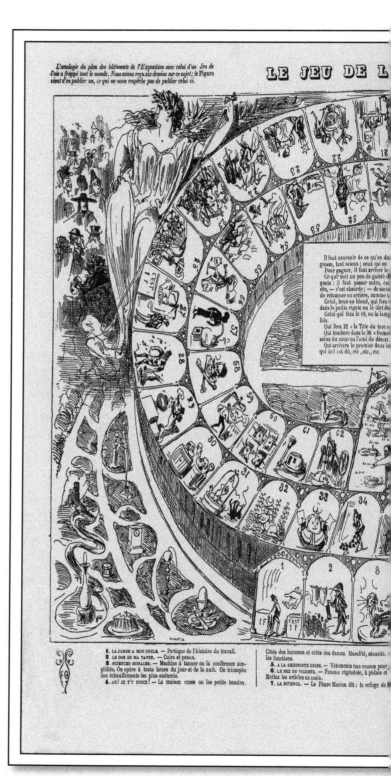

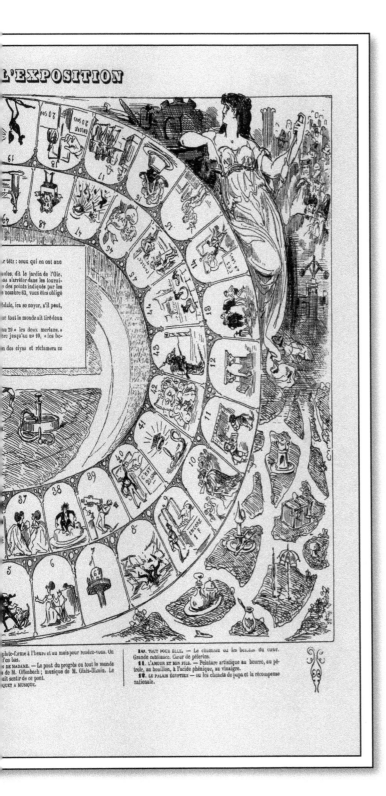

L'EXPOSITION

ar tête : ceux qui en ont une
ules, dit le jardin de l'Oie,
as s'arrêter dans les tourni-
e des points indiqués par les
nombre 63, vous êtes obligé

bdale, ira se noyer, s'il peut,
se tout le monde ait tiré deux
au 29 « les deux merlans, »
re jusqu'au no 10, « les bo-
n des oiyso et réclamera ce

plate-forme à l'heure et au mois pour rendez-vous. On
t en bas.
v DE MADAME. — Le pont du progrès où tout le monde
de M. Offenbach ; musique de M. Glais-Bizoin. Le
ait sentir de ce pont.
QUET A MUSIQUE.

10. TOUT POUR ELLE. — Le chapeau où les besoins du cœur.
Grande confiance. Cœur de pèlerins.
11. L'AMOUR ET SON FILS. — Peinture artistique au beurre, au pé-
trole, au bouillon, à l'acide phénique, au vinaigre.
12. LE PALAIS ÉGYPTIEN — où les chants de papa et la récompense
nationale.

The *Universal Exhibition of Art and Industry* was hosted in Paris in 1867, by command of Napoleon III. The goal was to overshadow London's International Exhibition of 1862, which hadn't lived up to the success of the Great Exhibition of 1851. The chosen venue was the Champ de Mars, France's premier military parade ground. Erected on it was the main building, shaped as a rectangle with rounded corners, spanning nearly 500 meters (1,640 feet) in length. This primary structure was surrounded by several concentric, similarly shaped smaller rings. The design's resemblance to the layout of the traditional French Game of the Goose was quickly noted. Consequently, it wasn't surprising when multiple Parisian publications depicted the exhibition using the Goose game motif. An illustration from the magazine *La Vie Parisienne*, which accompanies this passage, was paired with articles discussing the exhibition – some of which were quite critical. A point of contention was the entry fee, humorously echoed in the game. The first rule sarcastically states that players begin with a stake of one franc; if one can afford more, all the better; if less, too unfortunate! The game's starting square depicts a large, avaricious hand exacting this fee from an attendee.

REGLEMENT.

De spelers verdeelen zich in twee partijen, waarvan de eene partij speelt van No. 1 tot No. 63 langs de roode en de andere in omgekeerde richting langs de blauwe lijn, daarna bepaalt men den inzet en die de hoogste oogen werpt speelt het eerst. — Die als eersten worp 5 en 4 gooit gaat onmiddelijk op Koetsier, en die 6 en 3 gooit op Conducteur. — Die op een paardenkop

TRAMWAY SPEL.

VAN HOUTEN'S CACAO

J. VLIEGER - AMSTERDAM.

170

The *Tramway* game debuted around 1855 in France and quickly gained popularity, resulting in numerous editions across different countries. What distinguishes this Dutch edition and makes it revolutionary is the signboard on the tram: *Van Houten's Cacao*, which showcases the advertising slogan 'best and cheapest in use.' This slogan replaces the destination board seen in earlier versions. The game, a two-track variant of the Game of Goose, is played by two competing teams. The 'red' team follows one track, while the 'blue' team takes the other. Favorable goose-type spaces are marked by horse heads. Traditional hazards are reimagined as issues one might encounter on the tramway. For instance, the space representing *death* in the original game now becomes the 'wrong track' at 32 red/31 blue, where two trams face a head-on collision. The game's *prison* and *well* challenges are depicted as the 'bridge' at 6/57 and 'crossing' at 41/22. In these spots, players must wait until an opponent from the other team releases them. Such waits at single-track bridges or crossing points likely mirrored real-life experiences. The classic delays of the *inn* and *labyrinth* spaces also find their parallels: the tram 'derails' at 19/44, and 'fresh horses' are required at 52/11. These clever adaptations made for an engaging and realistic gameplay. Over the years, the Tramway game continued to enjoy popularity, even updating to incorporate advancements like electrification.

Van Houten's Drinking Chocolate Game.

Weesp: Van Houten

1889

Much like the *Game of the Tramway*, the *Drinking Chocolate Game* promoted Van Houten's product, drawing its foundation from the classic Game of Goose. In the original game, spaces favored by a goose were marked by distinct images of the Van Houten Cacao tin in this adaptation. In another marketing twist, the nonspecific playing spaces echoed the same advertising slogan found in the *Tramway* game. To strengthen the promotional message, traditional hazard spaces were tailored to the brand: the *bridge* at space 6 depicted Weesp, a city in North Holland and home to the Van Houten factory still to this day. Illustrations of the city 'before' and 'due to' Van Houten graced the sheet's lower corners. The *inn* at 19 transitioned into a cafe, and the *well* at 31 showcased one of Van Houten's advertising trams. The *prison* at 52 detained 'counterfeiters' of the product, while the *death* space at 58 presented a coffee pot, indicating players had to restart the game due to their 'recklessness' in choosing such an unhealthy drink.

Game of the Baby Jumeau Dolls. Paris: Jumeau 1889

The track of the *Game of the Baby Jumeau Dolls* unfolds on a large depiction of the Eiffel Tower, concluding at its pinnacle. The exhibition that the game commemorates occurred during a time when pro-American sentiment was high in Paris, evidenced by the dual flags crowning the sheet and New York's Statue of Liberty faintly outlined in the background. The game sheet also highlights the achievements of the Jumeau company: 'The expansive and elegant factory in Montreuil, birthplace of the Jumeau Dolls, now spans 65,000 square feet and boasts a workforce of 1,000...' Crafted from bisque and adorned in the intricate fashions of the era, their dolls were indeed treasures. However, they carried a hefty price tag and faced stiff competition from more affordable German imports. This rivalry is starkly depicted in the game. Spaces favorable to players, marked by the traditional Goose numbers, are graced by images of the Jumeau dolls. In contrast, the hazard spaces carry a distinct theme. The most striking is the *death* space at 58, showcasing a shattered German doll; the *prison* space at 52 confines another, shedding sorrowful tears; and yet another German doll is stranded in the well at 31, awaiting rescue. Although the company has since shuttered, Jumeau dolls remain coveted treasures among collectors today, with the rarest fetching five-figure sums.

Goose Game of General Boulanger. Paris: Figaro 1889

The illustration displays the opening page of the full-color supplement commissioned by *Le Figaro* and crafted by Imagerie Pellerin. The artwork was done by Gaston Lucq, who went by the moniker Glucq, a renowned Parisian designer. Starting from the late 1880s, Charles Pellerin collaborated with him to create contemporary advertising and political visuals. Below a dynamic depiction of politicians from the General's party gleefully dancing arm-in-arm is the Goose Game dedicated to General Boulanger. The game spans 63 spaces, with the goose markers showcasing the general. At the victory square, he's depicted donning an imperial crown and clad in ermine robes. The obstacles allude to significant episodes from his vibrant life journey. For instance, the 2nd space denotes July 14 (Bastille Day) and commemorates the general reinstating the customary military parades on that date during his tenure as the Minister of War. The 6th space, labeled 'lost portfolio,' alludes to his dismissal and subsequent relocation to the town of Clermont Ferrand by a government apprehensive of his burgeoning fame. His exit from the Gare de Lyon (12th space: proceed to the 44th space, Gare de Clermont) is highlighted. A throng of 10,000 supporters plastered the train with posters proclaiming, 'He will return!' True to the statement, the 44th space instructs players to 'Return to 12 (Gare de Lyon).' The game likely evoked chuckles from its players — maybe the most impactful mode of political influence?

LE GÉNÉRAL   BOULANGER

REVUE DU 14 JUILLET 1886

Commandant la division d'occupation de la Tunisie, il pacifie les tribus arabes. — Février 1884.

RÈGLE DU JEU DE L'OIE DU GÉNÉRAL

Game of La Couronne Gas Mantles. Paris: Robert and Co.

about 1900

This amusingly drawn game advertises the *La Couronne* brand of gas mantles, which were a major source of lighting before electric lights took over in the early 20th century. The modern gas mantle was developed by Carl Auer von Welsbach, a German scientist who in 1891 refined a mix of rare-earth oxides that, when heated by burning gas, emitted a strong white light from a fairly durable mantle. The game consistently highlights the benefits of gas lighting over older methods - and indeed the advantages of La Couronne mantles over their rivals. On space 7, labeled 'the good buy,' it shows a pack of La Couronne mantles, prompting you to double your roll. An accident due to a faulty mantle is depicted on space 31, showcasing its dramatic consequences and sending you back to purchase a superior product. Gas mantles were known to suddenly fall apart, often with a loud pop, so the dramatization isn't far-fetched. Many of the human figures in the game humorously adopt the cone shape of the mantle. It's also interesting to see how gas mantles were produced and used.

Game of Bisleri Ferro-China tonic. Milan: Bisleri about 1900

Bisleri's Ferro-China was crafted by Felice Bislieri, who, besides producing liqueurs, was also a pharmacist and a patriot under Garibaldi. The game promoting the Ferro-China tonic follows the classic Game of the Goose structure, with advantageous spaces doubling your roll in the exact same sequence. These spaces feature a lion's head – the brand's emblem. Two lions face off over a bridge at space 6, while the *prison* at space 52 transforms into a lion's cage. The *well* at space 31 displays the factory from 1881 located in via Savona, right in the heart of Milan - which only recently shut down and was converted into residential units. The traditional *death* space at 58 now shows a sick person. If you land here, you must buy a glass of Ferro-China and restart the game. The red bands along the track are adorned with promotional slogans for the tonic. Want to always feel energetic? Have a Ferro-China before eating. Wish for robust kids? To maintain your appetite? To sleep soundly? Or to stay healthy while traveling? Remember to pack your Ferro-China!

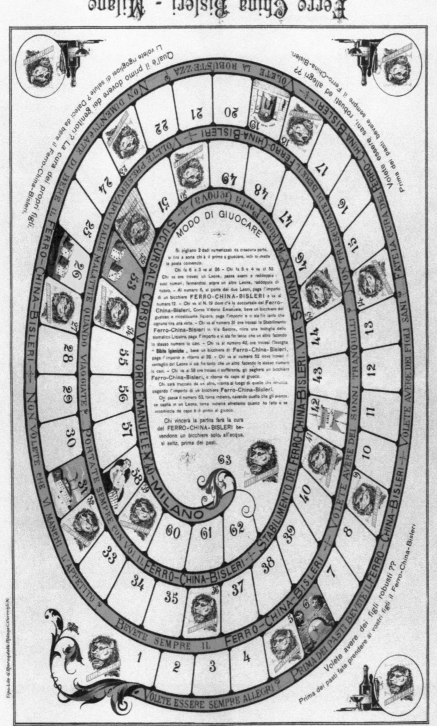

The Circuit of the Galeries Lafayette.
Paris: Galeries Lafayette
about 1906

T he era of aviation was just beginning when *The Circuit of the Galeries Lafayette* game was released. After their first flight in 1903, the Wright Brothers worked tirelessly to create a practical airplane. The result was showcased in the game – a Wright Flyer III from 1905. Though the plane could manage sustained flights lasting close to an hour, the incredible feats in the game were pure imagination. Yet, some of this fantasy became reality in 1912 when the store announced a challenge with a prize of 25,000 francs to anyone able to safely land on its rooftop. This feat was finally achieved in 1919 by a French pilot, Jules Védrines, with his Caudron G.3 biplane. Although he won the prize, he was also fined for breaking air traffic rules. The game itself is light-hearted – there's no *death* space, even with the risks of early flight, and a visit to St. Peter on space 51 seems rather pleasant. Advertisements for the *Galeries Lafayette* mainly show its international branches, both in Europe and abroad.

Goose Game of Carillon de Flandres chicory. Bourbourg, France Nord: Vilain Frères about 1910

Carillon de Flandres was a chicory brand from northern France made by the Vilain brothers. The game is packaged in boxes adorned with a unique bell-tower logo. Surprisingly, the game lacks targeted product ads, both in the illustrations and the rules, which strictly adhere to the Game of the Goose format. The special spaces that double your roll are marked with a goose and follow a single sequence, spaced by nine, rather than the classic game's dual sequence. Every space has some kind of illustration. For example, space 7 features a monoplane, likely representing the famed Blériot XI, the first to cross the English Channel in 1909. Other non-active spaces depict various subjects, so kids would likely enjoy identifying them. Straying from the usual illustration, space 42 usually portrays the *Labyrinth*. Here, however, the space depicts a rugged mountain range – where it's equally easy to get lost – instructing players to return to space 30. It's debatable whether children would be disturbed by the final image of a goose hanging by its neck, reminiscent of a poultry shop display.

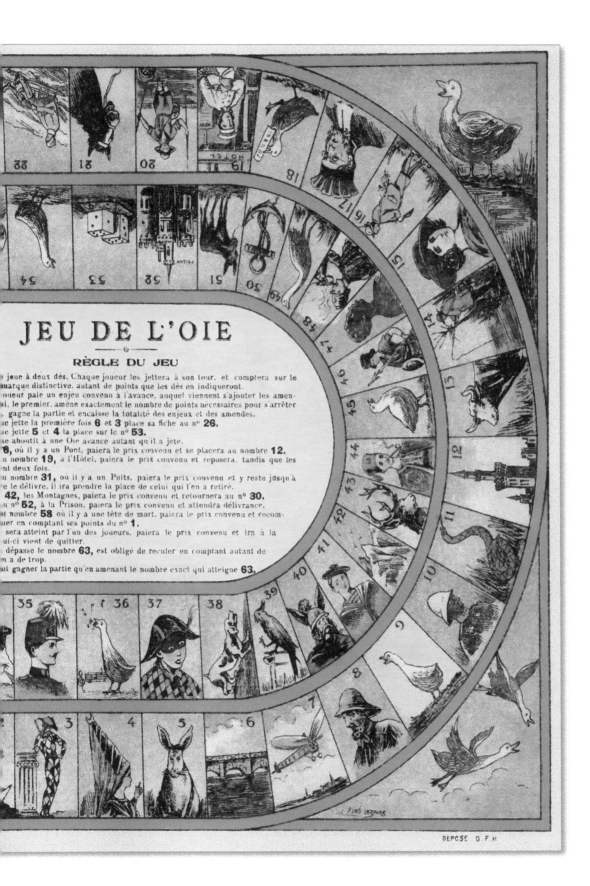

JEU DE L'OIE

RÈGLE DU JEU

n joue à deux dés. Chaque joueur les jettera à son tour, et comptera sur le marque distinctive, autant de points que les dés en indiqueront.

oueur paie un enjeu convenu à l'avance, auquel viennent s'ajouter les amen-ai, le premier, amène exactement le nombre de points nécessaires pour s'arrêter gagne la partie et encaisse la totalité des enjeux et des amendes.

e jette la première fois **6** et **3** place sa fiche au n° **26**.

e jette **5** et **4** la place sur le n° **53**.

e aboutit à une Oie avance autant qu'il a jeté.

6, où il y a un Pont, paiera le prix convenu et se placera au nombre **12**.

u nombre **19**, à l'Hôtel, paiera le prix convenu et reposera, tandis que les t deux fois.

u nombre **31**, où il y a un Puits, paiera le prix convenu et y reste jusqu'à re le délivre, il ira prendre la place de celui qui l'en a retiré.

42, les Montagnes, paiera le prix convenu et retournera au n° **30**.

u n° **52**, à la Prison, paiera le prix convenu et attendra délivrance.

ui nombre **58** où il y a une tête de mort, paiera le prix convenu et recom-uer en comptant ses points du n° **1**.

sera atteint par l'un des joueurs, paiera le prix convenu et ira à la ui-ci vient de quitter.

dépasse le nombre **63**, est obligé de reculer en comptant autant de a de trop.

ut gagner la partie qu'en amenant le nombre exact qui atteigne **63**.

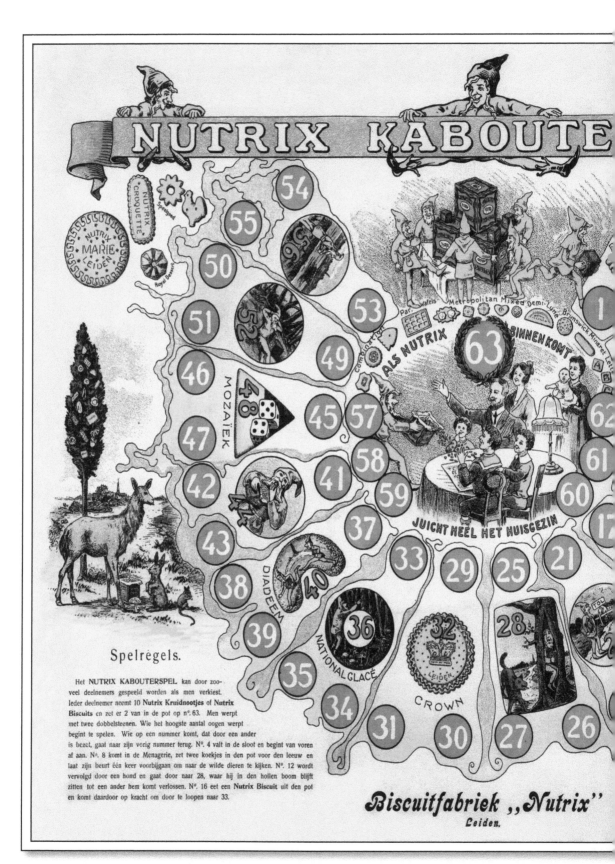

NUTRIX KABOUTE

Spelregels.

Het NUTRIX KABOUTERSPEL kan door zooveel deelnemers gespeeld worden als men verkiest.
Ieder deelnemer neemt 10 **Nutrix Kruidnootjes** of **Nutrix
Biscuits** en zet er 2 van in de pot op n°. 63. Men werpt
met twee dobbelsteenen. Wie het hoogste aantal oogen werpt
begint te spelen. Wie op een nummer komt, dat door een ander
is bezet, gaat naar zijn vorig nummer terug. N°. 4 valt in de sloot en begint van voren
af aan. N°. 8 komt in de Menagerie, zet twee koekjes in den pot voor den leeuw en
laat zijn beurt één keer voorbijgaan om naar de wilde dieren te kijken. N°. 12 wordt
vervolgd door een hond en gaat door naar 28, waar hij in den hollen boom blijft
zitten tot een ander hem komt verlossen. N°. 16 eet een **Nutrix Biscuit** uit den pot
en komt daardoor op kracht om door te loopen naar 33.

Biscuitfabriek ,,Nutrix"
Leiden.

SPEL

Boomstam

Klaverblad

Sigaar

Curaçao amandel

Frou-Frou

3

6

MENAGERIE

8

7

ALGERIA

10

12

11

16

14

EIWITBISCUIT

15

18

19

N°. 20 rijdt mee op een boerenwagen en betaalt 2 koekjes voor vracht. N°. 24 moet een
koekje voor tolgeld geven. N°. 32 eet een koekje
uit den pot en gaat naar n°. 37. N°. 36 is ver-
dwaald in het bosch en gaat terug naar n° 10.
N°. 40 wordt achterhaald en laat tweemaal zijn
beurt voorbijgaan. N°. 44 eet twee **Nutrix
Biscuits** en begint opnieuw. N°. 47 betaalt
een biscuit en mag negen punten vooruit. N°. 52
slaap gevallen, betaalt twee koekjes voor straf, en laat tweemaal zijn beurt
ijgaan. N°. 56 kan niet over het water, betaalt twee koekjes aan den pot
at met het bootje naar n°. 57.
e n°. 63 bereikt wint het spel en mag alle **Nutrix koekjes** hebben.

*Game of Nutrix Dwarves.
Leiden: Nutrix Biscuit Factory
about 1930*

Dutch games advertising cookies often used cookies as stakes. A prime example is this *Game of Nutrix Dwarves*, which takes players on a fairy tale journey filled with whimsical delights and challenges. Each player starts with ten Nutrix cookies, specifically the kind called *Kruidnoten* (a spicy treat traditionally linked with the *Sinterklaas* holiday in the Netherlands) and places two of these in the pot. Throughout the game, various kinds of cookies are showcased and named. At space 8, the Menagerie Lion cookie is integrated into the rules: 'Place two cookies in the pot for the Lion and pause a turn to watch the wild animals.' At different points, players are instructed to eat a cookie from the pot. However, a penalty (at space 44, which displays a gnome avidly munching through a big box of cookies) requires players to consume two from their own stash — and restart the game. The center space states: 'When Nutrix arrives, the whole family rejoices.' The first to reach this space can claim all the Nutrix cookies.

Board Games Go to America: the Quest for the New

The first board games printed in the USA were imports from London, and the earliest American productions in the 1820s were map games based on English models. Even the famous Mansion of Happiness game, often perceived as an American innovation, closely mirrored a London original.

One of the first games advertised in America was the Journey through Europe, created by John Jeffreys in 1759, previously discussed in Chapter 3. It was featured in a 1775 Pennsylvania newspaper as part of an ad for a diverse cargo of goods, ranging from hunting knives and cockspurs to silver shoe buckles. By the early 19th century, ads for English games regularly appeared in major cities: New York, Boston, Washington, and Pennsylvania. The range available in New York paralleled what was offered in London. The emphasis was on 'new' games, particularly around Christmas and New Year's. An ad in the New York Evening Post on December 31, 1810, showcased: Juvenile Pastimes, played with Totum and Counters, including Game of the Jew, Pastora,

Magic Ring, Bulwark of Britannia, Reward of Merit, Game of Human Life, Elegant Amusements, and Geographical Games of Europe, England, and the world. These ads didn't highlight the Game of the Goose, likely because it was deemed old-fashioned for the American audience.

The earliest American-made games were geographical ones, clearly inspired by English map-based games. Two publishers released strikingly similar games in 1822. F and R Lockwood from New York introduced the Travelers' Tour of the United States, showcased in this chapter. The other contender for the first American game is Edward Parker's The Geographical Pastime or Complete Tour of Europe, of which only one copy survives. Its exact release date remains uncertain, making it hard to determine which came first.

Between 1830 to 1860, a vast number of British immigrants moved to the United States, finding work in agriculture, mining, and major industrial hubs in New England and the Mid-Atlantic coast. At least one British manufacturer saw the opportunity to create a game introducing them to their new homeland. This game, titled *The Star-Spangled Banner, or Emigrants to the United States*, offers beautifully detailed depictions of the Eastern U.S., capturing the country's essence before the 1850s Californian gold rush.

The Mansion of Happiness, a game both instructive and entertaining, was the first American-produced game to make a significant mark. W. & S. B. Ives published the inaugural U.S. edition in 1843 in Salem, MA. It was reprinted multiple times by Ives and later by Parker Brothers in 1894. Although their claim of it being 'the first board game ever published in America' was later refuted, the game remains a pivotal moment in the U.S. board game history. The Game of the Goose, in contrast, had a minor impact, even though it had a few American editions around 1850.

Jules Verne's novel, *The Testament of an Eccentric*, exemplified the deep cultural ties between Western Europe and the United States.

It imagines the heirs to a Chicago millionaire's fortune participating in a grandiose Goose game played across America. Verne's more renowned work, *Around the World in Eighty Days*, indirectly sparked another board game called *Nellie Bly*, recounting her global journey where she outpaced the novel's fictional deadline. Another prominent European novel, *Robinson Crusoe*, led to a vividly lithographed game by Milton Bradley in the late 19th century.

Reflecting the American ethos was the game of the Errand Boy, highlighting opportunities for those from modest backgrounds. The game underscores virtues essential for success in the American Dream: honesty, dedication, and intelligence. Yet, victory in this context meant accumulating enough wealth to become a 'Honorable and Respected Banker & a Good Citizen' - a goal that might raise eyebrows today. Meanwhile, for the Shop Boy, a simpler game from that era, 'success' just meant getting to work behind the counter rather than cleaning the shop floor.

The Travelers'
Tour through the
United States.
New York: Lockwood
1822

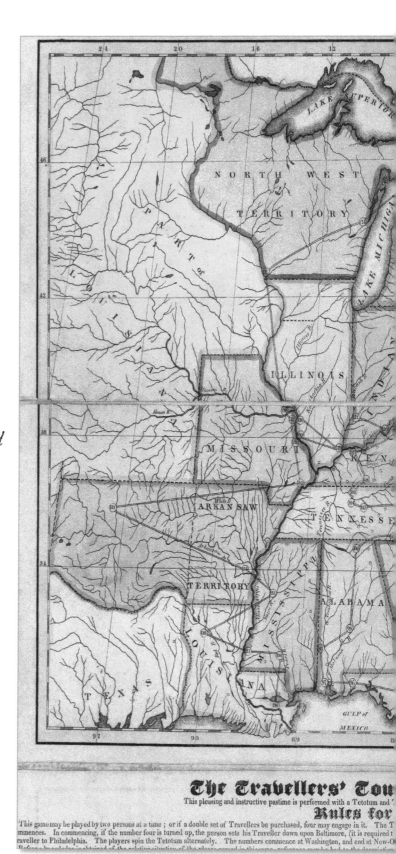

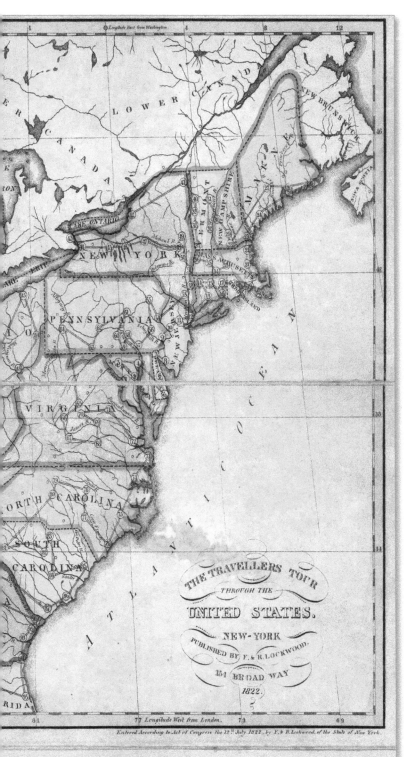

The *Travelers' Tour through the United States* features a map of the Eastern states, extending only as far west as the border of Arkansas Territory. The route, marked by numbered circles, starts in Washington, D.C., and concludes in New Orleans, which is the winning spot at number 139. The game's rules provide a list of locations corresponding to these circles, accompanied by a short description and, for cities, their population count. The map doesn't label these places, which is what makes the game intriguing. Players are challenged to identify the locations they land on without peeking at the rules. To up the ante, players could decide to also state the population of each location or else forfeit their turn. Most location descriptions are factual, such as: 'New York is the premier commercial city in America. The customs revenue from this port alone constitutes about a quarter of the entire U.S. revenue.' However, some descriptions offer charming insights, like: 'Charleston's residents (spot 86) are known for their refined manners and genuine hospitality.'

Game of the Star-Spangled Banner, or Emigrants to the United States. London: Wallis

1830

This captivating game, spread across 147 spaces, kicks off with the Great Sea Serpent 'lifting its head as high as a ship's topmast' and wraps up in New York City. Instead of dice or a teetotum, players draw numbered cards from a bag, which, according to the rulebook, makes the game 'more engaging.' State Capitals allow an additional turn with the explanation: 'Note that since each state governs independently and can't be directed from Washington, D.C.,... anyone landing on one of these spaces gets the advantage of drawing again right away.' Some spaces come with detailed directions, like:

- Space 10: *Turkey Buzzard* — This bird dines on dead animals and, when threatened, spews its stomach contents at its aggressor... *Move out of its path and start over*.
- Space 20: *Settler's Hut* — Constructed from logs and circled by a stake fence. *Pause one draw to experience it.*
- Space 44: *WASHINGTON* — The heart of national governance... The city has ambitious designs but mainly boasts a handful of modest structures, along with the Post Office, Bank, and a majestic Capitol or House of Representatives... *Advance to No. 73.*
- Space 90: *Lynch Law* (Arkansas) — A deplorable act, unfortunately too common in states far from the central government. It's nothing short of a travesty of justice... *Retreat to No. 67 (Woodcutter's hut).*

This game provides a vivid picture of how dramatically America has evolved over two centuries.

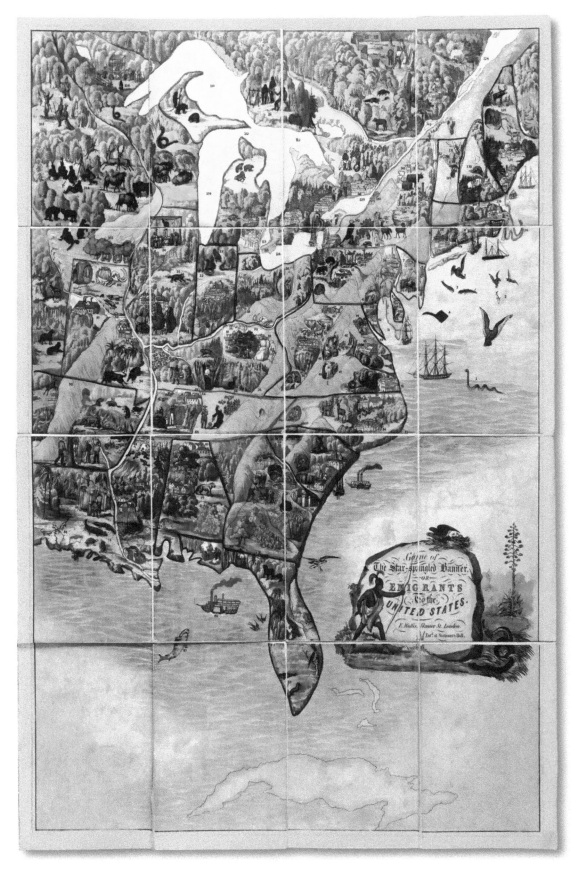

Game of The Star-spangled Banner, OR EMIGRANTS to the UNITED STATES.

193

The Mansion of Happiness. First published Salem MA 1843, this edition Salem & Boston: Ives, 1864

*T*he *Mansion of Happiness* game first hit the shelves in London in 1800, courtesy of Robert Laurie and James Whittle. Instead of spaces that doubled throws, the game featured a sequence of spaces propelling players six steps closer to the winning spot, showcasing the Mansion of Happiness. These spaces highlighted virtues like Piety, Honesty, Sobriety, and Gratitude. However, the rules specified that landing on vices such as Audacity, Cruelty, Immodesty, or Ingratitude meant a player 'had to backtrack to their previous spot and couldn't even contemplate happiness, let alone attain it.' The American versions kept most of these elements, with a few alterations. English references to the London jails Bridewell and Newgate were swapped out for the House of Correction (on space 30) and the Prison (on space 50). Interestingly, there's no penalty for landing on these jail spaces, but players could be sent there for specific infractions, like if a player lands on space 57, they're branded a robber and must serve two months in prison (meaning they skip two turns). However, they can get an early release if another player gets incarcerated. One notable distinction is that the U.S. version of the game didn't involve any gambling. The makers probably deemed gambling unfitting for a game that espoused lofty moral ideals.

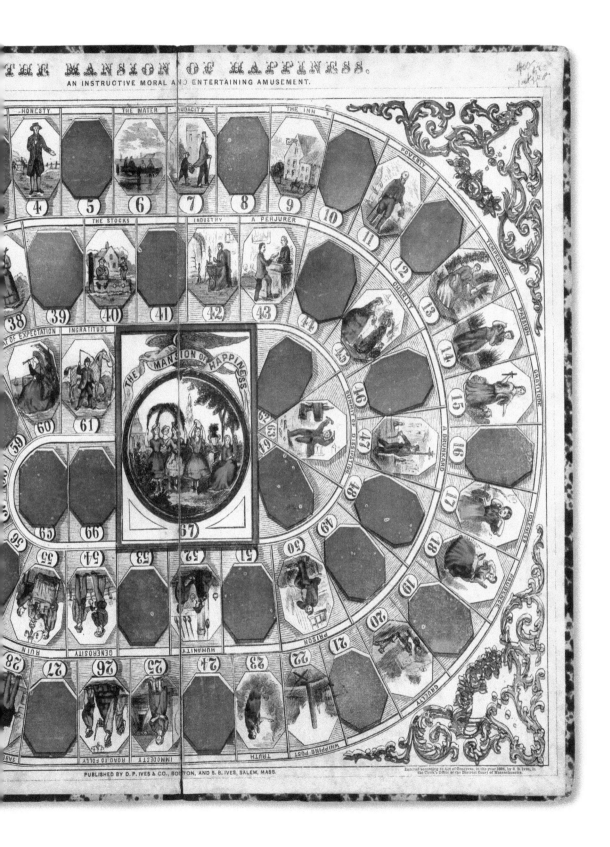

THE MANSION OF HAPPINESS.

AN INSTRUCTIVE MORAL AND ENTERTAINING AMUSEMENT.

PUBLISHED BY D. P. IVES & CO., BOSTON, AND S. B. IVES, SALEM, MASS.

Entered according to Act of Congress, in the year 1864, by S. B. Ives, in the Clerk's Office of the District Court of Massachusetts.

Game of Goose. Designed by Mary D. Carroll. Providence RI: Knowles, Anthony 1855

Classic versions of the *Game of the Goose* are a rare find in the U.S. The version copyrighted by Mary D. Carroll in Rhode Island in 1855 isn't the first instance of the Game of the Goose being published in the States. Earlier in 1851, J. P. Beach from New York City released the *Jolly Game of Goose*, modeling its design after an English original – except he used the shape of a goose and flipped it. Even though Mary Carroll's version largely sticks to the typical Game of the Goose format, it deviates by excluding the geese usually found on spaces 5 and 9. This absence can be seen in several English variants of the game, hinting that Carroll might've drawn inspiration from an English version. Yet, the delightful rural illustration in the final space, featuring bees buzzing joyfully around a hive, feels uniquely American, likely symbolizing the settler's dream.

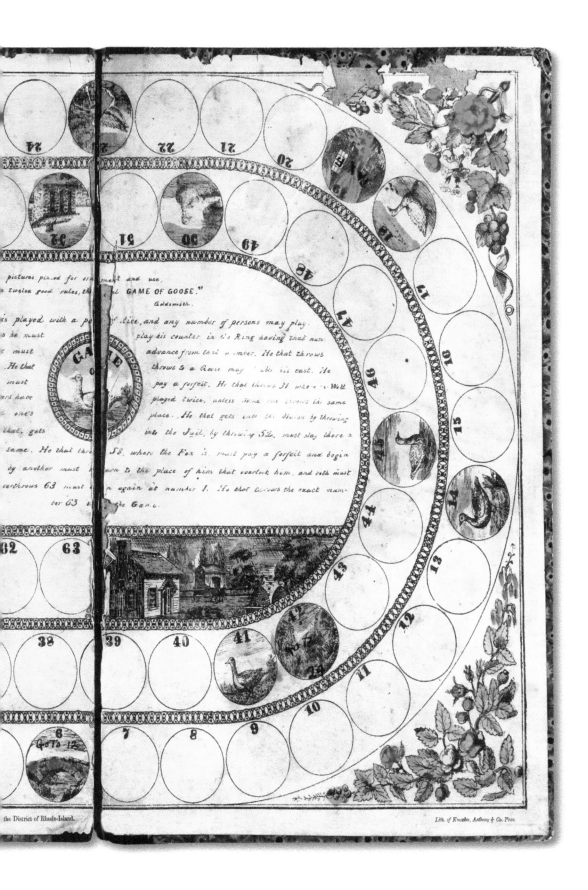

pictures placed for ornament and use,
... twelve good rules, th... GAME OF GOOSE."
Goldsmith.

...played with a p... of dice, and any number of persons may play.
...he must ... play his counter in the Ring having that num-
... must ... advance from that number. He that throws
... He that ... throws to a Goose may ... able his cast. He
... must ... pay a forfeit. He that throws 31 where ...Well
... have ... played twice, unless some one throws the same
... one's ... place. He that gets into the ... by throwing
... that gets ... into the Jail, by throwing 52, must stay there a...
same. He that th... 58, where the Fox is, must pay a forfeit and begin
by another must ... own to the place of him that overtook him, and both must
...verthrows 63 must ... again at number 1. He that throws the exact number 63 wi... the Game.

LE NOBLE JEU DES ÉTATS-UNIS

RENOUVELÉ
— DU NOBLE JEU DE L'OIE
RENOUVELÉ DES GRE

Qui amène 9 par 6 et 3, va à la case 26.
Qui amène 9 par 5 et 4 va à la case 53.

Qui va à la case 6, Etat de New-York, (le Pont, du Jeu de l'Oie), paie une prime simple et va à la case 12.

Qui va à la case 52, Missouri, (la Prison), paie une prime triple et attend qu'un autre partenaire vienne prendre sa place.

G. de Ribaucourt.

198

The Noble Game of the United States of America. Designed by Jules Verne. Paris: Hetzel 1899

Jules Verne's novel, *The Testament of an Eccentric*, revolves around the eccentric millionaire William J. Hypperbone. In his will, Hypperbone decrees that his massive $60 million fortune will go to whoever wins an elaborate game of Goose. The participants must journey through the states and territories of the U.S., moving according to dice throws made at the attorney's office. The novel delves deep into their adventures, offering a plethora of travel details. An included fold-out game depicts the U.S., where the states and territories are represented by their official seals. The game's design creatively mirrors the traditional Goose game. Every *goose* space showcases Illinois, recognized by its state seal that features the American eagle. New York, a fitting choice, stands as the *bridge* at space 6. The *prison* at space 52 represents Missouri, which was known for the infamous Missouri State Penitentiary in Jefferson City – the world's largest prison during that period. The ominous *death* space at 58 depicts California, hinting at a potential trip to Death Valley. Lastly, the victorious space at 63 once more highlights Illinois, signifying the attorney's office in Chicago where the game concludes.

Nellie Bly.

New York: Singer

about 1898

nlike the fictional characters in the earlier game, Nellie Bly was very real, although that was just her pen name. She was born Elizabeth Cochrane Seaman in 1864 and became a prominent American journalist. She managed to convince her editor at the *New York World* to let her attempt to outdo the fictional journey of Phileas Fogg in *Around the World in Eighty Days*. The game tracks her daily progress, starting in Hoboken, NJ, on November 14, 1889. She embarked on the ocean liner *Augusta Victoria*, heading for Southampton, England. By day nine, she was in Amiens, meeting Jules Verne in person. Her trip took her through the Suez Canal on day 13, and she continued to Hong Kong and Japan. The last sea journey was aboard the Oceanic, but storms delayed the ship, making it reach San Francisco two days late. However, Joseph Pulitzer, the owner of the *New York World*, arranged for a private train to speedily bring her back to New York. This record-setting train, which averaged an impressive 37 mph on its cross-country run and took precedence over other rail traffic, is featured in the game's centerpiece. Although the train did make stops in small towns for publicity, the journey's total time, a little over 72 days, held the record for only a short while.

Robinson Crusoe. Springfield MA: Milton Bradley

about 1900

Milton Bradley stands as a pioneering figure in the evolution of board games in America. Trained as a draftsman and lithographer, in 1860 he introduced *The Checkered Game of Life*, branching out from his primary lithography work. The game, themed around morality, was a revelation. Bradley's advancements in lithography meant the game could be produced in bulk without breaking the bank. A decade later, in 1870, Bradley rolled out a game inspired by Daniel Defoe's timeless novel, *Robinson Crusoe*. The version presented here bears a note on the back of the board, signaling it as an 'improved' edition. Its design is a parallel track game, where each of the four distinct tracks is undertaken by a separate player. Each journey begins from one of the board's corners. Some spaces have black stars denoting them as hazards – be it *storms, calms, breakers,* or *stiff breezes*. To ensure fairness, every track has an identical length and faces the same number of challenges, although the sequence of these challenges varies between tracks. A major pull of this dice-driven game is undoubtedly its visually stunning lithography, especially the vibrant border art.

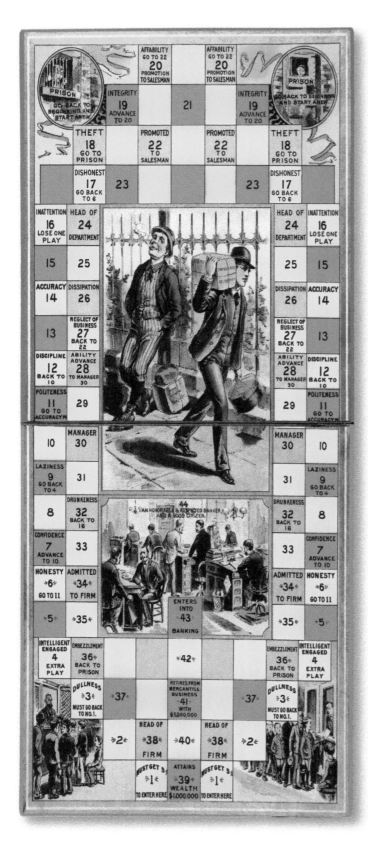

Errand Boy. New York: McLoughlin Brothers 1891

The McLoughlin Brothers, established in 1858, stand as arguably the pioneering force behind American board game companies. They crafted some of the most visually captivating games ever seen in the United States. The company's zenith was in the 1880s and 1890s, before Milton Bradley acquired them in 1920. The game highlighted here traces the journey of a modest Errand Boy, who ultimately becomes a Banker upon reaching space 43, clinching the game's victory. Players have the option to commence their journey on either side of the board as the initial track is doubled. As the game unfolds, the Errand Boy can ascend through various ranks, transitioning into roles such as Salesman (space 22), Department Head (space 24), Manager (space 30), Firm Partner (space 34), and Firm Leader (space 38). Reaching a net worth of $1 million is marked by space 39. The pinnacle of success is retiring from the business world with a whopping $5 million (space 41), making the player eligible to become a Banker at the triumphant space 44. Landing on virtues like Honesty, Politeness, and Accuracy can expedite a player's progress. In contrast, pitfalls like Laziness or Inattention can hinder or even reverse one's progress. The gravest threats are being incarcerated for Theft (space 18) or Embezzlement (space 36). To escape, players need a spin of 5, but even then, they must begin anew.

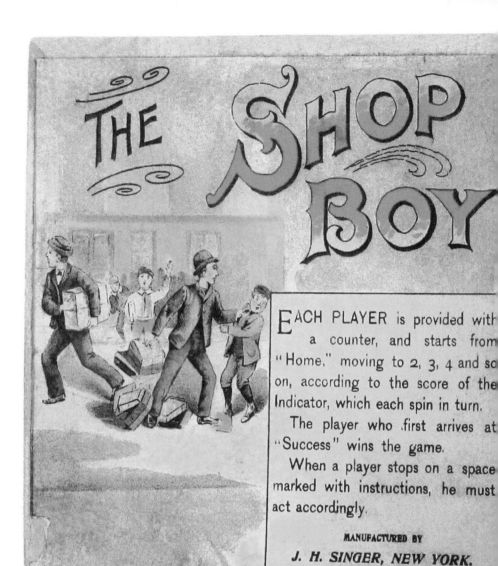

THE SHOP BOY

EACH PLAYER is provided with a counter, and starts from "Home," moving to 2, 3, 4 and so on, according to the score of the Indicator, which each spin in turn.

The player who first arrives at "Success" wins the game.

When a player stops on a space marked with instructions, he must act accordingly.

MANUFACTURED BY

J. H. SINGER, NEW YORK.

Shop Boy. New York: Singer 1890s

15	14	13	12	11	10 EARLY GO TO 18	9	8
16 LATE ⟶ HOME	39	38	37	36	35	34 HONESTY GO TO 41	7
17	40 PROMPT GO TO CASHIER	51		CASHIER 50	33		6
18	41				32		5
19	42				31		4 START AGAIN
20	43 TEMPER GO TO CHURCH	52 LOSE NEXT TURN	53 SUCCESS	49	SALESMAN 30		3
21	44	45	46	47 TIRED GO TO BED	48	29 SLOW GO TO 17	2
22	23 GOOD BOY GO TO SALESMAN	24	25	26	27	28	HOME 1

This particular game offers a glimpse into how board games were presented at more affordable price points in the United States. A vibrant game sheet was affixed to the base of a box, and the lid would feature another alluring image to entice potential buyers. For many American collectors, it's often the box lid that's the crown jewel, even more than the game itself. The depicted box lid presents boys of varying ages, delivering packages – a likely initial job for numerous youngsters of that era. One illustration portrays the ever-looming fear of dropping a package on the street. Originally, the game was accompanied by a spinner instead of dice. Regrettably, the showcased example no longer has its spinning arrow. The spinner's maximum value being four suggests a relatively leisurely pace when compared to the rapid tempo set by the dual dice in the Goose game. The game's messages would have resonated deeply with the youth in employment. Phrases like 'late – go home' were probably all too familiar. And while the 'tired – go to bed' reprimand might seem unusually compassionate for an employer, the inviting image of a bed at space 19 makes it conceivable.

Biography

Adrian Seville is a renowned expert in the cultural history of printed board games, having delivered lectures on his findings across both Europe and the United States. A Cambridge and Edinburgh University alumnus, Seville later joined City University in London, serving as the Academic Registrar. His 2016 board game exhibition at New York's Grolier Club garnered significant attention, with the Wall Street Journal lauding it as 'a mind-opening cultural event.'

Photo credits

All the images are by Adrian Seville except the following:

page 151 Bibliothèque nationale de France

page 173 Courtesy of Atlas van Stolk, Rotterdam

page 190 Courtesy of Daniel Crouch Rare Books

Editorial project **VALERIA MANFERTO DE FABIANIS**
Editorial coordination **GIORGIA RAINERI**
Graphic design **MARIA CUCCHI**

Copyright © 2023 / Adrian Seville

Originally Published by WhiteStar, s.r.l.
World English language edition by Mango Publishing Group, a division of Mango Media Inc.

Cover, Layout & Design: Dataworks

For permission requests, please contact the publisher at:

Mango Publishing Group
2850 Douglas Road, 2nd Floor
Coral Gables, FL 33134 USA
info@mango.bz

For special orders, quantity sales, course adoptions and corporate sales, please email the publisher at sales@mango.bz. For trade and wholesale sales, please contact Ingram Publisher Services at customer. service@ingramcontent.com or +1.800.509.4887.

The Book of Vintage Board Games: History and Entertainment from the Late 18th to the Beginning of the 20th Century

ISBN (pb) 978-1-68481-390-2 (hc) 978-1-68481-391-9 (e) 978-1-68481-392-6
LCCN: has been requested
BISAC: GAM001000, GAMES & ACTIVITIES / Board Games

Printed in the United States of America